Asperger Syndrome and Bullying

also by Nick Dubin

Being Bullied
Strategies and Solutions for People with Asperger's Syndrome
DVD
ISBN 978 1 84310 843 6

Asperger Syndrome and Employment
A Personal Guide to Succeeding at Work
Featuring Gail Hawkins
DVD
ISBN 978 1 84310 849 8

of related interest

Bully Blocking
How to Help Children who are Teased or Bullied
Revised Edition
Evelyn M. Field
ISBN 978 1 84310 554 1

Stop the Bullying
A Handbook for Schools
Ken Rigby
ISBN 978 1 84310 070 6

New Perspectives on Bullying
Ken Rigby
ISBN 978 1 85302 872 4

Bullying in Schools
And What to Do about it
Ken Rigby
ISBN 978 1 85302 455 9

Freaks, Geeks and Asperger Syndrome
A User Guide to Adolescence
Luke Jackson
Foreword by Tony Attwood
ISBN 978 1 84310 098 0

The Complete Guide to Asperger's Syndrome
Tony Attwood
ISBN 978 1 84310 495 7

Asperger Syndrome and Bullying

Strategies and Solutions

Nick Dubin

Foreword by Michael John Carley

Jessica Kingsley Publishers
London and Philadelphia

First published in 2007
by Jessica Kingsley Publishers
116 Pentonville Road
London N1 9JB, UK
and
400 Market Street, Suite 400
Philadelphia, PA 19106, USA

www.jkp.com

Library of Congress Cataloging in Publication Data
Dubin, Nick.
Asperger syndrome and bullying : strategies and solutions / Nick Dubin ; foreword by Michael John Carley.
p. cm.
Includes bibliographical references and index.
ISBN 978-1-84310-846-7 (pbk.)
1. Asperger's syndrome--Social aspects. 2. Bullying in schools. 3. Bullying in the workplace. I. Title.
RC553.A88D83 2007
362.196'85882--dc22
2006101043

British Library Cataloguing in Publication Data
A CIP catalogue record for this book is available from the British Library

ISBN 978 1 84310 846 7

Printed and bound in the United States by
Thomson-Shore, 7300 Joy Road, Dexter, MI 48130

To my parents, Larry and Kitty Dubin

Acknowledgments

Special thanks to the following people and organizations: Dr. Janet Graetz for being my mentor, the Michigan School of Professional Psychology for supporting me academically, Julia Press for her spiritual friendship, Steve Jones (my editor) for being such a pleasure to work with, Jessica Kingsley and her publishing company for suggesting and believing in this book, Michael John Carley for writing the Foreword, Laurel Hoekman and Christy Gast of the Gray Center for their overall support and encouragement, Dr. John Milanovich for setting me on my path, and Gail Hawkins for her support and encouragement of my work. Also, special thanks to my colleague and friend, Katie Kramer, for her insights in reading this manuscript, and to Barbara Bloom, for her support and help in the editing process.

Contents

Foreword

Remember those semi-satisfying days when we imagined that all bullies eventually suffered? That they grew up wasting inside because they knew what they'd done? I do. Back then, we welcomed those fantasies of social predators transported as adults into dead-end jobs and multiple divorces. As perhaps our only coping mechanism, victims and their families embraced the idea that the prior transgressions of bullies had corrupted their hearts so badly that good fortune was impossible.

Recent studies, however, tell a different story: that most bullies grow up to get good jobs, have healthy families, and are often thought of highly in their communities.

Ouch. How did *that* happen?

For starters, it wasn't just the bullies that were responsible. Back then, the social environment in which the bullying flourished was never held accountable or even considered—no one thought to look outside the bullies. Yet the environment in which the bullying existed played a significant role in the transgressions, and only now are we becoming somewhat aware of what really happened. Teachers, neighbors, even parents it turns out, were also culpable, and through our collective ignorance, they escaped blame for the enabling they unwillingly may have provided the instigators. Based on fears of their own perhaps, these accomplices, like the bullies, may also have wanted that "different" kid coerced by any means possible to conform to the status quo of behavioral acceptability. And therein they may have supported the bullying through varying degrees of visibility and intent.

These oversights came at a huge cost, for the victims, especially those on the autism spectrum, have often carried their trauma well into adulthood. I'm no doctor, but my experience in a prior profession (working for a veterans' organization) gave me experience in spotting Post-Traumatic Stress Disorder (PTSD). And as the head of GRASP (the Global and Regional Asperger Syndrome Partnership), the largest organization of adults on the autism spectrum in the world, I have been amazed to find low levels of PTSD as many times as I have in the autism spectrum individuals of our support group. As they recount bullied pasts, the fear is very often still alive in their eyes, and very much a presence in their lives.

It doesn't stop there. This trauma is further compounded by the internalized guilt that they feel for still hurting, so many years later. Having heard the mythical "Bullying is a part of life" speech ad nauseum (a fallacy perpetuated mostly by prior bullies), they feel even more inadequate for their inability to let the painful memories go. Their experiences, therefore, bad enough as they are, are also invalidated. Bullying has indeed been a nasty and highly neglected chapter in the book of Social Darwinism.

Yet if prior victims are to move on, let it go they must. These are years to which we can't return, and no apology will likely ever surface. Family love and family difficulties stay with us for our entire lives, but the pros and cons of childhood and school life have a designated endpoint—we don't leave our families, but we do leave school. The downside to this is that we usually don't receive closure for events that trouble and still confuse us.

One giant step that will influence the capacity towards letting go, however, is to eliminate the confusion of how and why these incidents transpired. Cognitively understanding what motivates the bullies, the adults in charge of supervision, or the ineffectual bystanders goes a long way towards making sense of these memories. And Nick Dubin's book will herein help enormously. Not only will *Asperger Syndrome and Bullying: Strategies and Solutions* help former victims piece together the "whys" and the "hows" of prior trauma, but educational professionals also are served well to read this book. For giving them much to choose from, Dubin meticulously outlines (and provides commentary on) every available community-based strategy and school program designed to combat those atmospheres that condone bullying. He has drawn from nearly all the applicable research, and woven the results into his writing to emphasize appropriate points. His book is a wonderful addition to the growing literature currently investigating the environment of bullying, the culture of bullying, and the myths we once believed about it.

But there's another component to this book—and it is one that isn't easy to read: Nick Dubin, a fellow spectrumite, was the victim of relentless bullying himself, and he writes in great detail about his experiences. *Asperger Syndrome and Bullying: Strategies and Solutions* serves as a great sociological analysis, yes, but readers are provided with an added layer—seeing a writer heal before our eyes. Knowing Nick personally, as I do, did not help me as I read. For Nick Dubin, not yet 30, was invited onto GRASP's Advisory Board very quickly because he is such a positive, outgoing and gregarious young man with a brain. I therefore found it stunning, and hard, to experience how much he'd been through.

Bullying is not an acceptable part of growing up. There may always be status, a hierarchy, or a social pecking order in our world, but it doesn't have to come at such a cost. We who are diagnosed on the autism spectrum can live, and thrive, within such very natural forces as competition, or the instincts of self-preservation. And we can learn about social rank through cognitive means. But it is when these forces are circumvented or taken past their appropriate endpoint that they then can evolve into bullying, a culture that contains no redeeming value for anyone involved.

The autism world once got an awful lot wrong. Admitting past mistakes (hard as it is) is a requisite precursor to our devising new and more effective ideas to make, for example, bullying a thing of the past. This sequence of events is the very nature of social progress, and it is reflected well through a selfless young man; now professionally dedicated to making sure others don't suffer the same horrors as he.

Michael John Carley, Executive Director of GRASP,
The Global and Regional Asperger Syndrome Partnership, Brooklyn, New York

Introduction

If you are an adult reading this book and you know a child with Asperger Syndrome, I'm going to ask you to try a little exercise. I want you to imagine that the moment you arrive at work in the morning, a co-worker calls you an idiot. Ten minutes later, as you are minding your own business, another co-worker sticks his leg out as you are walking by and trips you. You fall to the floor and a bunch of your fellow employees begin laughing and making fun of you. Later on that day, you are summoned in by your boss and he accuses you of being lazy even though you are trying your hardest.

Now, what if you had to experience this type of work environment every day of the week? How long do you think you would stay at this job? My hunch is not long. And yet, children with Asperger's and others who experience bullying on a regular basis do not have the luxury of choosing to leave. They cannot opt out of going to school like an adult who can choose to switch jobs.

There is a real crisis today when it comes to the bullying of vulnerable populations of children. As you will learn in this book, children on the autism spectrum are an extremely vulnerable population. I have written this book in order to provide real strategies and solutions to combat and even reverse this incredibly destructive behavioral trend.

I once learned about a principle in quantum physics that I found fascinating. I believe it's an apt metaphor for how bullying affects a person's self-esteem from childhood into adulthood. The principle I am referring to is called entanglement. Essentially, it was discovered that if you take two particles and separate them to the ends of the universe, their behavior patterns will be identical. The information between the two particles seems to exceed the speed of light so that there is almost this "psychic" connection between them. Albert Einstein called entanglement "spooky action at a distance" (McTaggart 2003, p.11).

When I hear adults with Asperger Syndrome talk about the sadness and pain that is still present in their lives from having been bullied as children, it reminds me of entanglement. The painful memories of the past become entangled with the present even though bullying is no longer taking place. One's behavior in the present may mirror how one would have reacted 20 or 30 years ago, even though the circumstances of one's life may be totally different. This is clearly spooky action at a distance. One 30-year-old man with Asperger's I met, who was routinely bullied as a child, told me how he still gets paranoid about people being out to "get" him, even though he knows rationally this is not the case. It truly is a form of Post-Traumatic Stress Disorder. When a person is subjected to humiliation on a daily basis in childhood, it is very difficult not to be affected by those past experiences in adulthood.

The consequences of not dealing with bullying, especially with a vulnerable population, can be disastrous. And yet, bullying is ignored all too frequently. How often have you heard people say the following?

> Being bullied will toughen him up. He's going to have to enter the
> "real" world someday, and people can be cruel. Better he gets used
> to it now. He's got to learn to stand up for himself.

Unfortunately, these statements are patently false. Being bullied does not toughen someone up. As you will learn, being bullied does the opposite of toughening a person up. It actually wounds the soul, destroys the psyche and ultimately, in some cases, can lead to suicide. We would try to curtail any behavior that might eventually cause a death, such as smoking, drinking, and drug abuse, but the consequences of bullying can be just as serious. It's time that we begin to recognize this truth.

It is everyone's responsibility to curtail the bullying problem. A good bullying prevention program in schools should not only involve faculty, but parents and peers as well. The power of peer intervention, in fact, will be one of the main thrusts of this book.

I don't believe I chose to become involved with this issue. I believe the issue chose me. I had no intention of becoming involved in bullying prevention until one fateful day about a year and a half ago. While watching a television program one afternoon, I came across a renowned children's author, Patricia Polacco, who was speaking to a group of school children. I had no idea who she was, but her style of speaking intrigued me, so I decided to keep watching. After about five minutes, she began talking about the cruelty she experienced at the hands of bullies from her childhood and how it affected her to this day. As I was watching, memories of the many experiences I had being bullied began to flood my psyche. I became overwhelmed by a sense of sadness. I began crying as these episodes played themselves out in my mind's eye.

As I heard Ms. Polacco describe how these episodes have stayed with her to this day, I could see that the children in the audience were absorbed by what she said. They seemed to "get it." Here was this woman the children clearly looked up to, and she was standing there sharing her deepest vulnerabilities with them. One could sense that the children were awestruck by her self-disclosures. Then Ms. Polacco said something that I will never forget. "From now on, if you choose to bully other children in this school, look out! For it will no longer be 'cool' for you to do so. Bullies, be on alert! The bystanders are on the march."

I was mesmerized by this statement. I thought to myself, "How cool it would be if I could do what she's doing." In that instant, I realized that speaking and writing about bullying would be one of my callings in life.

I was diagnosed with Asperger Syndrome in 2004. As an adult with Asperger's, I can now understand how vulnerable a target I was for being bullied as a child. I do not want any child to have to go through the daily humiliation I repeatedly endured throughout my childhood.

I detail below some sobering statistics:

- One study revealed that parents of 22 out of 22 children with Asperger's, ages 11–19, reported that their children were being victimized by peers (Konstantareas 2005).

- Average victimization among that group of children was 1.25 times a week (Konstantareas 2005).

- Twenty-three percent of the parents in that same study reported frequent victimization (two or more times) per week (Konstantareas 2005).

- Another study interviewing 400 parents of children with ASD, ages ranging from 4 to 17, found that 94 percent had been bullied or victimized (Heinrichs 2003).

- Children with ASD are four times more likely to be bullied than their peers (Little 2002).

- One hundred and sixty thousand children miss school on a daily basis because they are afraid of being bullied or harassed (Fried and Fried 1996; Gray 2003).

- Children have a 75 percent chance of being bullied throughout their school years from kindergarten to twelfth grade (Hoover and Oliver 1996).

- In 1993, 27 percent of middle-school students worldwide reported often being bullied (Smith and Whitney 1993).

- Almost everyone is excluded and ostracized by their peers at some point in time. Peer rejection or exclusion is a covert form of bullying.

What are some of the after-effects of having been bullied?

- Low self-esteem in adulthood.

- Problems interacting with the opposite sex. Gilmartin (1987) found that 80 percent of heterosexual men who had been repeatedly bullied in school had trouble progressing beyond casual interactions with women.

- Lower academic performance (Hazler, Hoover, and Oliver 1993a).

- Increased depression.

- Lower immune system performance leading to various diseases (Ross and Ross 1988). This makes sense as people who have to direct all their energy toward defending themselves will eventually run on empty.

- Anxiety. Dorothea Ross says (2003, p.76), "Fear permeates their [victims] everyday life and for many children, becomes an ingrained response."

- Suicide.

These alarming statistics clearly establish that the problem of bullying must be addressed. In their book *Bullycide: Death at Playtime* (2001), Neil Marr and Tim Field report that children frequently do not tell adults that they are being bullied. The book chronicles various "bullycides" (suicides that are a result of being bullied) that happened from 1967 to the present in the United Kingdom. This information is a wake-up call to the issue of bullying.

This book is written from the heart. It is my plea to educators, parents, and students to recognize that bullying is a subject that deserves considerable attention, especially with regards to vulnerable populations like children on the autism spectrum. More than anything, this book is a call to action.

All of the names (and initials) that appear in this book either are pseudonyms or describe fictitious people unless otherwise noted, such as in the Acknowledgments section.

Chapter 1

My Own Experiences of Being Bullied

A young boy with Asperger's Syndrome once said to me, "I just don't know why bullying was ever invented." Unfortunately, I don't think this child's inquiry will ever be adequately answered. We are both human and animal, carrying the predatory instincts we share with our animal friends. However, I believe our goal as a species should be to rise above these destructive impulses. As higher-order beings, it is *morality* that differentiates us from all other creatures that walk the earth.

Morality is a curious word these days. I certainly do not want to sound preachy by using it, but I believe the word is appropriate for our discussion. Since few people are willing to be the moral arbitrators on the subject of bullying, especially with regards to the Asperger population, I am glad to assume the role.

I believe anyone who ignores bullying is immoral. Growing up, I was all too often the victim of such nasty, preventable attacks and I want to do everything in my power to make sure vulnerable populations are protected from bullies.

The impact of bullying

It was a late August day in 2004, the day before my first day as a doctoral student in psychology at the Michigan School for Professional Psychology. I was a wreck. My mind was very much entangled with the past. Entering the building, I was afraid of being teased. I was sure I wouldn't fit in and everyone would notice it. I thought people would laugh at me, make fun of me, or, worse, ignore me. My fears were completely irrational. Why would adult students in a doctoral program, in psychology no less, act like this?

I think back to that day and realize my fears had nothing to do with this group of students who would be my classmates for the next four years. I had never even met them before. It was clear that I was suffering from a

Post-Traumatic Stress Disorder (PTSD) response that was triggered in me. This was not a new response for me. I had been having these kinds of PTSD episodes from childhood all the way through adulthood.

I once had a conversation with my grandmother that I found rather illuminating. My Grandma Clara is 88 years old and still remarkably sharp for her age. In talking to her about my role in bullying prevention with schools and agencies, she proceeded to tell me an interesting anecdote from her childhood:

> You know, Nick, this reminds me of something from when I was a schoolgirl. I remember that there was a girl who was constantly picking on me. It became so bad that I finally told the teacher. I'll never forget what the teacher's reply was: "Clara dear, 20 years from now, you won't remember this. Don't make such a big deal about it."

Clearly, her teacher was wrong. Not only does my grandmother still remember being bullied, she remembers the ignorant statement made by this particular teacher over 75 years ago. Unfortunately, too many teachers would say the same thing today. Being bullied is something that stays with you for life.

When I contemplated writing this book, I knew that it meant I had to take myself to a very sad place. In order for this book to have the maximum effect, I was going to have to tell all. I realized that the reader of this book would not understand my intentions for writing this book unless I disclosed these painful episodes of being bullied. That is part of my personal history. Therefore, this chapter will focus on those traumatic events.

First, I want to discuss incidents of bullying by a teacher or an employer because I believe these acts are the most traumatic type of bullying that exists. My definition of teacher and employer bullying is when persons of authority use their power to engage in a purposeful power struggle where the goal is not to help a person, but rather to demean him or her. In essence, when a person of authority bullies someone, it opens the door to condoning peer bullying.

Several personal instances of this type of bullying painfully come to mind.

Opening the door

I often speak at conferences on the subject of bullying, and the first incident is one I mention at every conference I speak at involving bullying prevention. It took place when I was a second grader at Pembroke Elementary School in Birmingham, Michigan.

The incident began in the Learning Resource Center (LRC) classroom where another girl and I were asked by our teacher to go down the hall to a second-grade classroom and remind a couple of other students who had forgotten to come to the LRC room that day. When we arrived at the room, we could see that the teacher was busy conducting a lesson. The other girl, who I will call Jennifer, suggested that I knock on the door rather than just barging in, so I followed her suggestion. The teacher, who I'll refer to as Mrs. B, waved her hand, signaling for us to come in. Jennifer told me to open the door. I tried turning the door handle but, for some reason, it seemed stuck and wouldn't open. After what seemed like 30 seconds, the teacher saw that we were still standing outside the door. I suppose Jennifer could have simply opened the door and made life easier on me, but she chose not to do so. Mrs. B was growing impatient. She walked over, opened the door, and said sarcastically in front of the whole class, "Didn't I say that you could come in?"

"Yes, you did," I said.

"Well then, what's the problem? I'm closing the door and I want you to open it."

Once again, I tried opening the door without any success. At this point, I could see that other kids in the class were laughing at me.

"Mrs. B, I can't open the door."

"That's absurd. How old are you?"

"Eight years old," I said.

"You are eight years old, in the second grade, and you're telling me that you can't open a door?"

"I can't open this door. It won't open," I said timidly.

"This is ridiculous. Jennifer, I'm going to close the door and I want you to open it," Mrs. B said. By this time, I was completely humiliated, but I was somewhat relieved that she asked Jennifer to open the door. I was convinced that at least I would not be the only one who Mrs. B was going to embarrass. I fully expected that Jennifer would try opening the door and would fail as miserably as I did. Much to my surprise, the strangest thing happened. Jennifer opened the door with ease.

"See!" said Mrs. B. "You saw her open the door. Now, you open this door right now. This instant! You're eight years old. Now start acting like it." At this point, my jaw dropped to the floor. There wasn't something wrong with the door after all. There was something wrong with...me. In that moment, my whole perception of reality was turned upside down.

Once again I tried my best to open the door without any success. I was sweating while the kids were now rolling on the ground laughing. I felt that this horrific moment would never end. As if things weren't bad enough, Mrs. B provided the fatal blow to this humiliating experience.

"Oh my goodness, I cannot believe my eyes! Jennifer, I want you to open this door again." Of course, she did. And, of course, I was wishing that I was invisible.

"Now look, I'm getting tired of this. If you think this is funny, it's not. And if you don't open this door right now, you are going to be in big trouble. Do you want to be suspended from school?"

"No," I said almost in a whisper.

"Then open this door immediately." I tried again and failed. For a third time, Mrs. B asked Jennifer to open the door. And, for a third time, she did. By now, everyone in the class was laughing hysterically, watching what was taking place.

"This is last time I'm going to tell you. Open this door."

I knew that no matter what I did, I wasn't going to open the door. It was locked as far as I was concerned. Jennifer had just found some secret way of opening it and I hated her for it. Realizing that I was going to suffer more humiliation, I ran down the hall all the way to the office. I was inconsolable. The secretary in the office tried to understand what happened to me, but I was emotionally out of control. I was hyperventilating, screaming, and crying.

I was still in the same emotional and physical state when my parents arrived at school. Eventually, I was able to articulate what happened, and they communicated this to the principal so that my "meltdown" made sense to him.

Years later I learned that the reason I couldn't open the door was because it was one of those knobs you had to turn counterclockwise. Being characteristically rigid as a person with Asperger's, I thought doorknobs could only be turned clockwise. When turning the handle clockwise did not work, it never even entered my mind that I needed to turn the knob counterclockwise. I could have been there for a week trying to open that door and I don't think I would have ever considered the possibility of turning the knob in the opposite direction. Jennifer was not smarter than me. Her thought processes were just more flexible.

Why did Mrs. B bully me? Most likely she thought I was challenging her authority. Because she somehow felt threatened by my behavior, her fight-or-flight mechanisms kicked in. Instead of simply trying to under-stand why I was having trouble opening the door, she made an incorrect assumption about my intention. In her mind, there was no reason an eight-year-old couldn't open a door, and the only reasonable explanation was that I was challenging her authority. The truth of the matter was that my Asperger's was causing me to behave rigidly. Instead of trying to figure out why I was having trouble opening the door, she got angry. All she had to do was show me that the knob had to be turned the other way, and I probably would not remember this incident as an adult some 20 years later.

As a result of Mrs. B's incorrect assumption, she committed the number one cardinal sin as a teacher. She bullied a student. She condoned bullying in front of an entire classroom. What a powerful message she sent to all of the other students who witnessed and perhaps even enjoyed watching this event.

Locked in the bathroom

In the summer of 1994, I received a phone call from a tennis instructor who I hadn't seen in several years. He had read my name in the latest Southeast Michigan Tennis Association (SEMTA) magazine where I was ranked number one in the division for boys age 16. Impressed with how I had risen in the ranks, Ron asked me if I would come and work for him during the summer as a tennis instructor at a nearby prestigious country club in Bloomfield Hills, Michigan. I was extremely flattered that he had called me and, without thinking twice, I accepted the job.

During the first week on the job, it seemed, at times, he was talking to me in a condescending way and I wondered if I was imagining things. It seemed as if I was being treated with less respect than my co-workers. I wasn't sure if he was just teasing me or ridiculing me. As the weeks went on, I began to realize that it wasn't my imagination. Ron started calling me the "waddler" because he thought the way I walked was like a duck with a waddle. Not only that, Ron encouraged the children who I was teaching to call me that. So it wasn't unusual for one of the children taking lessons to come up to me and say, "Hi, Waddler." Can you imagine how degrading that was for me?

Things only got worse. One day Ron totally stepped over the line. During one of the tennis lessons, I went to use the restroom facilities located beyond the tennis clubhouse. As I was in the bathroom, little did I know that Ron was scheming to demean me in front of all the children. Ron's plan was to have all the kids hold the door shut so I couldn't get out. I was struggling to open the door while ten children were trying to keep me trapped in the bathroom. To make a long story short, this prank went on for at least three minutes. By the time they finally let me out, I was so angry I left the club that day, went home and cried. Again, I was shaken to the core. It brought back memories of being in second grade when I couldn't open the door.

Besides these negative experiences with teachers, I also suffered needlessly as a result of my fellow classmates' unchecked behavior.

The handcuff incident

In 1987, I was a third grader at Pembroke Elementary School. One day, a classmate, Stewart, invited me to play with him and another boy, Ralph, after school. I was elated. After all, it wasn't every day that I got invited to play with someone. Stewart told me to meet them at a neighborhood park after school.

This park was situated right behind our house. Our backyard was literally on the outer edge of the park. This fact becomes important as it permitted my dad to save me from a dire situation. The park was empty at 3:30p.m. when I arrived. There was no sign of anyone. I wondered if Stewart and Ralph had forgotten about meeting me. I waited five or ten minutes and was about to leave when I saw Stewart and Ralph racing towards me on their bikes. I was once again elated that they hadn't forgotten about me, but the good feelings were short lived. Who would have suspected that these two had a plan that would cause me great humiliation?

Here's what happened: Stewart and Ralph asked me to come over to the swing set. Once there, Stewart said we were going to play a game of "cops and robbers" and that I should put both my arms up against the swing poles. Having no reason to believe that Stewart was trying to trick me, I cooperated. Stewart then proceeded to handcuff both my arms to the swing and, immediately thereafter, he and Ralph took off on their bikes. At first I thought they were going to just leave me there, but they decided to torture me. They began riding their bikes around the block shouting "sucker" every time they rode by the swing set, with me standing there completely helpless. I totally panicked and began shouting for them to come back. The more I screamed, the more they taunted me. The pressure of the handcuffs against my wrists was unbearable and the fact that I couldn't move terrified me. I wondered how long they would keep me there.

For about a half hour, I was in an empty park screaming my head off with no help forthcoming. I was hoping a police officer might drive by and see me. A neighbor. A mailman. Anyone! Most of all, I was hoping my parents would hear me. Eventually my father did. He had just come home from work when he heard me yelling in the park. As soon as he heard my hysterical screams, he rushed outside to see what was going on. Stewart and Ralph saw my dad running towards the park and immediately came to unlock the handcuffs. Stewart arrived at the swing set before my dad so he could purposefully create an explanation to give to my father. He said to me: "You'd better tell him we were playing cops and robbers. You're not a tattletale, are you, Nick?"

"What the hell is going on here?" my dad shouted.

"Nothing much," Stewart said. "We were just playing cops and robbers, weren't we Nick?" I didn't say anything.

"That's not what it looks like to me," my dad said.

"Yeah, we were playing cops and robbers," Ralph reassured my father. Again, I didn't say anything.

"Nick, is that true?" I was silent.

"Nick, I want you to come home right now."

I gladly abided by my dad's wishes. Once home, I told my father exactly what happened. As angry as my dad was about what happened to me, I think he felt worse that my so-called friends weren't my friends at all.

The next day something interesting happened. Stewart and Ralph were playing in the park and they saw me shooting baskets in my backyard. Probably because they knew my dad was angry with them, they came over and acted as if they were still my friends, and to see whether he believed the whole "cops and robbers" story. As soon as my father saw them coming, he came outside as angry as I've ever seen him. I'll never forget his words to Stewart and Ralph.

> Look, you two, if you guys want to be Nick's friend, that's one thing. But from what I saw yesterday, you two did just about the meanest thing I've ever seen done to someone. Stewart, I know your story about "cops and robbers" was a bunch of baloney. I'm not stupid, son. If you think that you can do this to Nick and get away with it, you're wrong. Now you are welcome to be Nick's friend, but you are not welcome to bully or abuse him. Do I make myself clear?

And then, do you know what Stewart and Ralph did? They immediately got on their bikes and rode away. They never asked me to play with them again, nor did they ever mess with me again.

Rain Man

I remember that I was once deeply hurt by a friend of mine who was a tennis buddy. My friend Jake, along with a friend of Jake's, and I were to room together at Oberlin Tennis Camp for a week. On the way to Oberlin, I remember commenting to Jake about the shape of various telephone poles as we were traveling along the highway. I was convinced that depending on the area code you were in, the shape of the telephone pole would look slightly different. Jake seemed interested in my thoughts, but it probably was just the appearance of interest.

Later on in the week, my friend Jake and his friend began calling me "Rain Man," in reference to Dustin Hoffman's character in the movie, *Rain Man*. I told them to knock it off but they wouldn't stop. Finally, I asked them why they were calling me that. Jake responded, "Anyone who's interested in telephone poles has got to have something in common with the Rain Man." It was a very hurtful statement. I couldn't understand why my friend was comparing me to someone who was autistic. It wasn't until 2004 that some of these mysterious questions I had been asking myself over the years began to resolve themselves through my Asperger Syndrome diagnosis.

The preacher

Around the time I was in high school, I started developing what I thought was a "comedic routine" known as "the preacher." Essentially, I imitated an evangelical reverend doing "call and response" with his congregation. This routine became so popular that, before I knew it, the whole high school was aware of it. Every day, people would come up to me and ask me to do "the preacher." It became a little tiresome after a while, but I didn't mind the attention. As a matter of fact, I thought that doing the routine would help make me popular. People would see how funny I was, and then they would want to be my friends. What I didn't realize was that these people were laughing at me, not with me.

Sometimes, kids would bully me into doing "the preacher." "C'mon Nick, you haven't done it for two weeks now. It's time." I felt that if I didn't perform, they wouldn't like me. "C'mon, why won't you do it? You're being stubborn. Everyone wants to see you do it! Nick, do it! Right now, or else! Do you want me to beat you up?"

Usually these threats were enough to make me comply. Sometimes, crowds of 20 or more would gather around me once the word spread that I was about to perform. Initially, doing "the preacher" seemed like a great

way to make friends but after a while it became a chore. By the time I gradu-
ated from high school, I had figured out that doing "the preacher" was not
the way to gain popularity as I had hoped.

Being ignored

I think excluding someone is a form of covert bullying. The tennis team I
was on in high school excluded me socially. Now in part, this was only
natural, since I did not share any of their interests, such as dating, drinking,
and partying. But now when I watch my senior high tennis banquet on
video, I notice something very interesting. No one spoke to me. At my
table, all the kids on my team were talking and joking around, but I was
totally excluded from all conversation. I certainly had difficulty socializing
with my peers, but no one was willing to help include me in the
conversation.

The really amazing thing about all this is that I was the number one
singles player on my varsity tennis team for all four years. I was the team
captain and had been designated "the most valuable player." I was the only
player designated as "All State." Logically, I should have been the most
popular kid on the team. I was the equivalent of the star quarterback of a
football team. However, I wasn't popular. I don't think I was disliked. I just
had nothing in common with my teammates other than our mutual interest
in tennis.

Why do I care?

The episodes I have just recounted are just a few examples of my daily
reality growing up. There were times when these incidents made me
contemplate suicide. Was life really worth living under these
circumstances? However, rather than seeking sympathy, I am trying to
make an important point: *most of these painful episodes could have been prevented.*
If there is nothing else you take away from this book, it is that bullying
prevention is possible, as will be detailed in the chapters on empowerment.

I hope it has become apparent why I am so passionate about bullying
prevention and those who are diagnosed with an autism spectrum disorder
(ASD). Because of how I am hard wired neurologically, I was an incredibly
easy target for all parties involved: teachers, employers, and peers. I have
been wounded deeply by all that has happened to me. For many years
during adolescence, I was afraid to be seen in public. I would never leave my
parents' house on weekends for fear that someone from school might see
me. I was constantly tormented by the thought of running into someone for

fear that person would ridicule me. More importantly, being bullied put me in a serious state of depression for many years. There were several times throughout my adolescence when I wanted to die. The thought of going to school every day and having to face those who would either ignore or make fun of me was often too much to bear.

The reason I have made bullying prevention one of my life's missions is because I do not want to see other children go through the same (or possibly worse) torment I endured when all of it could have been prevented. Though I am a much different person now than I was then, some of the "psychic scars" will be with me for life. These memories are, unfortunately, forever ingrained as a part of who I am.

It has become apparent to me, through the research that I have done and my own personal experiences, that bullying is a life-or-death issue. If we as a worldwide community do not respond to what is happening to our children, some of them will be permanently damaged or even attempt suicide (Field and Marr 2001). I feel fortunate now to be able to speak out on bullying. I have the knowledge and self-awareness to make sense of my past and understand the dangers of bullying. I can now use my life's energies to try to combat and eradicate bullying.

The rest of this book will focus specifically on defining the problem and finding solutions. To fully empower ourselves we need to understand why individuals on the autism spectrum are such easy targets for bullying.

Chapter 2

Easy Targets:
Children on the Autism Spectrum

Unfortunately, I grew up during a period when Asperger Syndrome was not recognized as a bona fide diagnosis. Even as late as the 1980s, autism was generally understood as a condition that often required institutionalization. It wasn't until individuals on the autism spectrum, such as Temple Grandin, Donna Williams, Stephen Shore, and Jerry Newport, came forward and shared their incredibly brave stories that Asperger Syndrome and High Functioning Autism finally became identified and understood.

It took 13 years between the time Lorna Wing, noted researcher on autism, wrote a paper recognizing Hans Asperger as the "father" of this syndrome, and when Asperger Syndrome was finally added to the *Diagnostic and Statistical Manual of Mental Disorders IV*. This addition took place in 1994 (Klin, Sparrow, and Volkmar 2000).

Asperger Syndrome has now become a topic of great interest. This interest may be due, in part, to recent statistics that suggest that one child in 150 (Center for Disease Control and Prevention 2007) is currently diagnosed as being on the autism spectrum. Educators, parents, social workers, and psychologists are now playing catch-up in trying to understand the qualities of these diagnosed individuals and how best to provide services, education, and care that is in their best interests. It is no surprise that, over the last decade, there has been much more information published about Asperger's and autism than in all of the preceding decades combined.

One thing we know for sure is that children on the autism spectrum are easy targets for being bullied. The severity of the impact that bullying has on these vulnerable victims is a problem of monumental proportion. It should be the goal of any caring adult, including teachers, administrators, and parents, to gain tools of empowerment toward solving this problem.

Chapters 3 to 8 will offer the reader those specific tools. For now, I will focus on the etiology as to why children with Asperger's are such easy targets for being bullied. Being an easy target does not mean that there is something wrong with them or that they are doing something to cause their victimization. Rather, the problem is the conduct of the bullies that will be discussed later.

What is Asperger Syndrome?

First, Asperger Syndrome:

- is not the same as Schizoid Personality Disorder, though there are some overlapping similarities (Wolff 1995)
- is not a character defect or the result of bad parenting (Attwood 1998)
- does not produce emotionless human beings.

Most difficulties that arise in daily living for a person with Asperger's can be traced back to Wing's (2001) Triad of Impairments.

The first, and perhaps most recognizable, impairment is in the domain of social interaction. Individuals with the syndrome tend to socialize in ways that society would deem unconventional or even inappropriate. Throughout this chapter, the root cause will be explored as to why people with Asperger's have a difficult time socially and how this contributes to making them easy targets for bullies.

The second impairment, which will be discussed in greater detail later on in the chapter, is in communication. Generally speaking, people with Asperger Syndrome have wonderful vocabularies and are extremely verbal but have a tendency to be verbose and one-sided while talking to another person. They may also have problems understanding some of the nuances of language when metaphors and figurative speech are being used. Intonation and pitch can vary a lot for people with Asperger's. Where one person may be very expressive, almost having a theatrical presence, another may speak in a monotone and sound like a dull college professor. Though the range of communication problems varies among individuals with Asperger's, the difficulties are usually present.

The last impairment Wing (2001) mentions in her work is one's thinking or processing. Individuals on the spectrum can exhibit stereotypical behaviors such as doing certain things in a repetitive manner or amassing an enormous amount of information on one or more subjects of interest, and these behaviors relate to this impairment. Another aspect of this impairment is the tendency to see things in black-and-white terms.

Along those same lines, people with Asperger's are also very trusting by nature because they rarely tell lies themselves. In being gullible by nature and taking others at their word, a person does not look at the gray of the situation.

I believe that people on the spectrum and with Asperger's view things in a cause-and-effect way, a formulistic way, if you will. "If A is true, then B must be true." Often, when a person with Asperger's believes that "A" is true, then "B" is *always* going to be true, without exception. If a person with Asperger's begins to trust a person, that person can sometimes take on exemplary status before he or she has truly earned it. The rationale goes something like this: if he is a nice person, he would never lie to me.

The key word in that sentence is "never." We all know that even nice people may lie on occasion. However, for the person with Asperger's, this type of scenario seems inconceivable. This could be classified as black-and-white thinking.

Many times throughout my childhood and adulthood, I tended to idealize people and put them in an angelic category. Similarly, people who didn't meet my expectations were put into an "all bad" category. If someone who I had idealized did something that I considered to be hurtful, he or she automatically went from the good category to the bad. No questions asked. One of the things I have had to learn over the years is that people are not all good or all bad. We all have varying shades of gray. This is an incredibly difficult concept for someone with Asperger Syndrome to understand.

The complexity of Asperger's

It is helpful to understand that Asperger Syndrome is a highly complex construct and not as easily understood as the *Diagnostic and Statistical Manual IV* would make it seem. Learning about the complexity of this syndrome helps to sensitize people to the vulnerabilities of someone with Asperger's and to better recognize how to provide protection for them against aggressive behavior from others.

Experts generally define Asperger Syndrome as a neurobiological disorder that manifests itself in impaired communication and emotional processing. These same experts talk about the many sensory processing differences and challenges that persons with Asperger's have to confront. While all of that is true, many professionals do not discuss or write much about the wide variance of traits among these people. It is entirely possible for two people with Asperger's to have totally different personality profiles, even though they share the same basic diagnosis. For example, people with Asperger's can either be introverts or extroverts, math wizards or have a learning disability in math. They can be athletes or computer geeks, skilled professionals or blue-collar workers. Because Asperger's spans such a wide continuum, there are myriad personal differences that can be observed among the Asperger population.

Perhaps these wide-ranging differences are what make the Asperger diagnosis so unique as a construct. The dichotomous and heterogeneous nature of this syndrome may help to account for the unique personalities displayed by a great number of people with Asperger's. However, one common thread is always there. They are easy targets for being bullied.

How serious is the problem?

There are conservative estimates from one study that indicate 94 percent of individuals with Asperger's will be bullied and/or victimized frequently (Heinrichs 2003). Another study found that 22 out of 22 individuals with autism spectrum disorders, ages 11–19, were being regularly victimized by their peers (Konstantareas 2005). Other studies report that this same group is four times more likely than their peers to be bullied (Little 2002). Olweus (1993) reiterated the fact that once individuals are selected as a "target," they are usually targeted repeatedly.

These statistics paint a rather bleak picture. To better understand the scope of the problem, it is necessary to appreciate the complex nature of Asperger Syndrome. Since there are many paradoxes and differences within Asperger's, the focus here will remain on the similarities and how each characteristic of Asperger's increases the probability of becoming an easy target for bullying.

Low frustration tolerance

One behavior that can be observed in most children with Asperger's is the inability to tolerate frustration. This trait is due to a combination of different factors. As mentioned earlier, sensory processes can be altered for the individual on the autism spectrum beyond the range of what most people would deem comfortable (Attwood 1998). These individuals can be hypersensitive to external stimuli, such as fluorescent lights, humming noises, or wearing certain types of clothing material that can cause great personal discomfort. Hypersensitivity can often be diffused by a calm environment, which helps to maintain a homeostatic or comfortable state of being.

Likewise, the individual who is hyposensitive to external stimuli, due to dull senses, may require constant sensory stimulation. This type of person may crave tactile, kinesthetic, and visual stimulation in order to stay physically regulated and balanced. Some individuals on the autism spectrum have hypotaste issues, where they need to be stimulated orally (Bogdashina 2005). This means that they might put foreign objects or substances into their mouths, like pencils or paper.

As a child with Asperger's enters elementary school, the environment becomes more unpredictable and tumultuous. Bells ring and fire alarms suddenly go off. Substitute teachers are not uncommon. The schedule may be interrupted because of a school assembly. On any given day, a school bus may be late or there may be a different driver. For the individual with low frustration tolerance, unpredictability is the enemy. Most people would hardly notice the changes that take place on a daily basis in school, but those same changes can easily throw a child with Asperger's into a panic. When frustration tolerance decreases, it is fertile ground for a *meltdown*, where one's behavior becomes inappropriate, disinhibited, and out of control.

How does low frustration tolerance increase the probability of becoming an easy target for bullying? Read the following story.

Eli is an eight-year-old boy with Asperger's. Every morning when he gets ready for school, he has trouble buttoning his shirt. He usually can button the first three buttons, but has a hard time with the last few. Eli exhibits a lot of his frustration by making grunting noises and calling himself names. "Idiot...ugggh, why can't I do this? I'm so sick of this."

His brother, Harry, hears this and teases him about it. "Eli, why are you being such a nerd? Quit acting so weird!"

At Eli's elementary school, they are having a fire drill today. However, for this fire drill, the principal did not come on the loud speaker to warn students in advance that the alarm would be going off. When the alarm does come on, it is a total shock to Eli's nervous system. He immediately puts his hands over his ears and begins exhibiting nervous head tics, and makes weird sounds while his head bobs from side to side. Once outside, Eli appears visibly upset. While all the other kids are glad to get out of class and go outdoors for a few minutes, Eli has a scared look on his face. His classmates notice his demeanor and come over to him. "Hey, look at Eli. What's the matter, scaredy cat? What are you doing with your head? You are such a total weirdo."

> Later on that day, Eli has math class. He is given a set of multiplication problems involving two-digit numbers. Once he has completed the assignment, he hands in his work. The teacher returns it and demands that Eli redo the assignment even though he answered all the problems correctly because he failed to show the computations that led to his correct answers. Eli is angry and tells his teacher, "This is such a stupid assignment. Why do I have to show my work on paper when I can do it all in my head?"
>
> "Because I said so, Eli. Can't you do just one thing without having to question the logic behind it?" the teacher replies.

Eli's low frustration tolerance increased his chances of being bullied in a number of ways. His perfectionist attitude automatically sets up an antagonistic confrontation between him and his teacher, which the other students observed. His difficulty in buttoning his shirt resulted in an emotional outburst that his brother teased him about. And his hypersensitivity to the fire alarm as well as the unpredictability of this occurrence made it easy for his classmates to target him on the playground. Remember, meltdowns make a person stand out! In fact, any unusual behavior will make a person more likely to become a target for bullying at school.

Monotropism

Well-known autism advocate Wendy Lawson (2005) talks frequently about the concept of individuals with autism spectrum disorders being monotropic by nature. Monotropism refers to a difference in executive functioning between neurotypicals (non-autistic people) and individuals with Asperger Syndrome.

To understand monotropism, it helps to be familiar with its counterpart, polytropism. Most people are polytropic by nature. Polytropic people have less difficulty multitasking than a monotropic person. They can perform a variety of tasks in succession without having difficulty switching gears between tasks. For example, an office secretary has to answer telephones while simultaneously greeting clients, getting coffee for the boss, scheduling appointments, typing memorandums, and performing other requested tasks. For a monotropic person, this type of workload would be virtually impossible because focusing on more than one activity at a time creates a mental overload.

Most school environments are polytropic in nature and do not cater well to the monotropic person. There are usually many transitions throughout the normal school day. Even in elementary school, students have multiple homework assignments that require them to shift focus from one subject to another.

Monotropic people tend to become handicapped in ordinary social situations. A monotropic person finds it much easier to focus on the details of any given situation rather than spreading his or her attention evenly over many different stimuli. In social situations, monotropism translates into missing the meaning or misinterpreting the context of a given communication, and instead focusing on and being able to process only part of the conversation. Also, polytropic people can more easily shift from topic to topic in a conversation. This inability to move comfortably from topic to topic can cause the conversation of someone with Asperger Syndrome to appear stiff and stilted. We will briefly review the concept of monotropism in our discussion regarding auditory processing difficulties later on in the chapter.

Let's see how this might relate to an individual becoming an easy target for being bullied.

Vern, a 14-year-old boy with Asperger Syndrome, has just arrived home from school. He looks at his Palm Pilot and notices that he has homework assignments in all seven classes that are due the next day. Then Vern's mom suddenly asks him to go to the supermarket around the block and pick up a few items for dinner. Vern becomes hysterical and has a mini-meltdown. "Oh c'mon Mom, please! Don't do this to me. I'm going crazy, don't make me do this!"

Vern's brother's friend comments later that day, "Vern, you'd think your mom asked you to go to Timbuktu. What's the big deal about going around the corner? Man, you are selfish."

The next day, Vern goes to school and remembers he only finished three of the seven assignments that were due today. In science class, the teacher asks for the biology homework that Vern forgot to do. Vern panics and has a meltdown in class. "Oh my God, where is it? Did I do this assignment? Oh my goodness, c'mon, where is it? I can't believe I didn't do it."

His teacher says, "Vern, this is the third assignment in a row that you have failed to turn in on time. I'm going to have to sit down and talk with your folks. You need to try a lot harder."

Later that day, a classmate taunts him. "Vern is a sped [short for special ed]… Vern is a sped." Other classmates begin laughing at Vern. Finally at lunch, Vern feels some relief from his anxiety when he is able to sit by himself in the cafeteria. However, after a while he begins to feel isolated and decides to go to another table and try to enter a conversation with some other students. Fortunately for Vern, no one asks him to leave, at least not immediately. His fellow students are engaged in conversation about the latest television program that everyone watched the night before. The discussion then shifts to the school dance this Friday. Then people start talking about Britney Spears. Then the conversation abruptly turns to the Superbowl. While everyone is talking about the Superbowl, Vern is still thinking about the school dance. Vern summons up the nerve to ask the group a question: "Hey, does everyone know who they're going with to the school dance?"

His classmates look annoyed and perturbed. "Dude, we're not talking about that anymore. You're a space cadet." They start laughing at him. Vern has no idea what he did wrong.

This story illustrates how Vern was judged negatively because of his monotropic nature. His weaknesses in social understanding were misperceived as him being spacey. Let's review the events of these two days. First, Vern was overwhelmed by the seven assignments that were all due the next day. On top of this, when his mother asked him to go to the store, it further lowered his frustration tolerance and caused a meltdown. A polytropic person could have more easily handled the seven assignments and would not have had a problem going to the store. The next day, Vern's frustration tolerance was challenged again when he was asked to turn in the biology assignment that he had forgotten to do. Because of Vern's perfectionist attitude and his internalized shame for not turning in the assignment, he had a meltdown in class. This appearance of immaturity made him a visible target later on in the day when he was repeatedly called "sped" by his classmates. Finally, Vern's delayed processing made him a target for being socially inept when he failed to keep up with the conversation. Monotropism made it hard for Vern to shift from topic to topic. He got "stuck" on one topic that was being discussed and wasn't able to shift to the next one. While everyone at the table was talking about the Superbowl, he was internally obsessing about the school dance. When Vern took a major social risk by entering the conversation, he ended up alienating the table full of students.

Motor difficulties

It is a well-known fact that people with Asperger Syndrome and those on the autism spectrum have difficulty with gross and fine motor skills. An individual who has motor difficulties will stand out in an unusual way to others. He may have trouble with handwriting, art projects, physical education, as well as activities in the playground. Let's take a look at Jimmy.

Jimmy is a nine-year-old boy with Asperger Syndrome. In physical education class, Jimmy is required to climb up the rope to the ceiling. He is the last in line. Everyone else in the class has no problem with this task. By the time it is Jimmy's turn, he is terrified. He knows that he can't do it, but is afraid to look like a total geek. When Jimmy tries and miserably fails, Jimmy's classmates capitalize on his vulnerability. "Jimmy, you belong in a girls' school, you wimp. You're pathetic. You couldn't even make it halfway up the rope."

Later that day, Jimmy is wandering around the playground while everyone else is playing. He finally decides to enter a game of soccer. The ball is passed to him and he kicks it directly to an opposing player. A few minutes later, he mistakenly kicks the ball in the wrong direction and scores a goal for the opposing team. A teammate approaches him and says, "We don't want you on our team anymore. You don't know what you're doing."

Now it is art class. Jimmy is asked to paint a picture of his family. Though he loves his family, he has terrible fine motor skills and can't paint anywhere near his age-appropriate level. His art teacher comes over and remarks, "Jimmy, I asked you to paint a picture of your family, and you're painting stick figures! Surely you can do better than this. I want you to redo this assignment!"

Gullibility

When I was a boy, I used to go to Tiger Stadium with my dad to see the Detroit Tigers baseball team. One time a friend of mine joined us. During the game, my friend jokingly told me that a particular ballplayer winked at me as he was running into the outfield. I believed him until he started to laugh and told me he was joking. Taking other people at their word is a nice quality to possess, but on occasion it can get people with Asperger's into trouble. Another example is Frank.

Frank is an eighth grader with Asperger Syndrome. During physical education class, Frank's classmates conspire to get him in trouble. They tell Frank that Ms. Watson, the gym teacher, asked him to go into the girls' locker room to get something out of one of the lockers. Frank complies. He goes in, only to hear a bunch of girls screaming. Before he knows it, he is down in the assistant principal's office being reprimanded for invading the girls' privacy.

Auditory processing delays

Imagine that you were being physically attacked. What would you do? Obviously, you would try to defend yourself. What if that wasn't possible? What if, every time you tried to defend yourself, there was a 10- or 15-second delay between your instinct to act and the time you threw your first punch? Wouldn't that put you at a great disadvantage?

That scenario is analogous to the way a child with Asperger Syndrome handles verbal abuse. Many children with Asperger's have auditory processing problems. Rapid-fire responses are almost impossible for them. Because their brains work in such a way where it takes a little longer to decode incoming communication, their response time will be slower. The effect of this delay is that one's ability to respond in a timely manner becomes impeded.

Though many individuals with Asperger's are monotropic, some have a hard time filtering out irrelevant information that comes in through non-auditory senses. In other words, a person becomes overstimulated from information overload. The stimuli coming in through other "sensory channels," such as sight, sound, and touch, interfere with the auditory channel.

Jake, a 13-year-old boy with Asperger's, has trouble with "comebacks" due to auditory and sensory screening issues.

Jake always seems to get picked on by his classmates. Ten minutes after he gets harassed, he realizes what he should have said, but by then it's too late. Jed is his biggest foe. Every day Jed calls Jake a bad name. Today, Jed calls him an idiot. As Jake is trying to formulate his "comeback," he notices his teacher yelling at a group of kids on the playground. He sees a group of girls playing hopscotch and becomes uncomfortable with how hot he feels. All of these observations and sensations are bombarding Jake, which distract his attention from selecting a "comeback" to say to Jed.

Unlike visual processing that can occur at a slower pace, auditory processing happens instantaneously. It is not surprising that children with Asperger's struggle in this regard. Later in the book, I will be talking about scripting and how it can help individuals with Asperger Syndrome verbally defend themselves.

Problems with reading non-verbal cues

Most individuals with Asperger Syndrome have problems with visual-spatial processing. The significance of this fact is that most non-verbal cues are decoded visually.

The main difference between reading the body language of another person and reading words on a page is that the former is ambiguous and the latter is not. This is why it is possible for someone with Asperger's to be a visual learner while simultaneously experiencing problems with visual-spatial processing. There is no fixed set of rules when reading non-verbal body language. It is an abstract way of taking in and processing information. Since 85 percent of communication is non-verbal (Young 1998), individuals with Asperger Syndrome are put at an incredible disadvantage in using social skills successfully.

Here's an illustration of how difficulty in reading body language can contribute to becoming an easy target for bullying.

Margarita is a 13-year-old girl with Asperger Syndrome. When one of her classmates says to her, "Margarita, we're just so glad you're here," she takes that statement literally. She doesn't notice that her classmate has her hands on her hips and is rolling her eyes. She doesn't observe that all the girls are rolling their eyes. She only hears the statement "We're just so glad you're here."

Margarita replies, "I'm glad I'm here too."

Special interests

Throughout the literature on Asperger's, one of the most commonly mentioned themes is the proclivity to develop certain special interests. A special interest is when a person accumulates a tremendous amount of knowledge about a given subject. These interests can seem quite ordinary, like learning almost every statistic and historical fact about baseball. On the other hand, the special interest can be esoteric, like knowing the map routes for every U.S. interstate highway or the statistics of every Grand Ole Opry show from 1930 to the present. What makes these special interests so significant is that they generally exclude learning about other interests including subjects relating to popular culture (movies, pop music, fashion). Also excluded might be subjects that must be learned in school. The individual becomes so focused, and perhaps obsessed, on one or two special interests that he or she tends to exclude almost all other possible interests.

When I was a boy, I knew where every expressway in the United States began and ended. I proudly used to tell other kids that the Interstate 90 expressway's eastern terminus is in Boston near Logan International Airport and that the western terminus is in Seattle. Looking back, I can see that sharing this information was not an ideal way to get the attention of kids with whom I wanted to be friends. But at the age of 12 or 13, I incorrectly thought I would impress others with the knowledge of my special interest because they would see how smart I was. Instead, I'm sure they just thought I was weird.

Lack of dating experience

International author and presenter Tony Attwood (1998) aptly remarks that when individuals with Asperger's reach high-school age, they are often perceived by their peers as being gay. The reason for this is simple. Many individuals with Asperger's, due to their delays in social development, have not yet begun to date. Around adolescence, when boys start to brag about how they are becoming sexually active, many individuals with Asperger's have not even experienced their first kiss. It should be noted that the majority of those with Asperger's are heterosexual, so the assumptions that their classmates might make about them will often be false.

As vulnerable as the autism population is for being bullied, the gay population is also a major target. If individuals with Asperger's are suspected of being gay because of a lack of experience in the dating arena, it can spell disaster.

Leon is an 18-year-old high-school student with Asperger Syndrome. He has never asked a girl on a date, although he has had crushes on several girls in his class. Because he is not sure how to act in certain social situations, Leon is afraid to risk displaying inappropriate social behavior towards girls. The senior prom is this weekend. Leon sees that all his classmates have dates lined up, except him. One of his classmates remarks, "Leon, you've never been to one school dance in four years. Are you gay or something?"

Another classmate chimes in, "Yeah Leon, I never see you hanging out with the ladies. What's with you?"

Leon quickly responds, "I'm not gay. What are you guys talking about?"

"Then how come we've never seen you with a girl? How come you've never had a girlfriend?"

Leon has been misperceived by his classmates. Though he is heterosexual, his peers think he is gay because they have never seen him with a girl. The reality of the situation is that Leon's social difficulties have prevented him from asking a girl out on a date. *What Leon's classmates are observing is his Asperger Syndrome, not his sexual orientation.* Yet being teased about his sexual orientation may create increased confusion about whether he really might be gay or not. If he becomes aware that he really is gay, then the teasing will only serve to magnify how unacceptable he will end up feeling around his peers.

Cultural illiteracy

Cultural illiteracy has to do with a person's inability or lack of motivation to understand what is happening in the current popular culture. As discussed earlier, the special interests of people with Asperger's are often esoteric and preclude other interests. If a boy is spending all his time studying insects, learning about Civil War battles, or reading Stephen Hawking, he hardly has the time necessary to care about the latest Kelly Clarkson music video. If the person with Asperger's lacks knowledge concerning pop culture, he or she is at a social disadvantage with peers. How did this issue impact Cindy? Read the following story.

Cindy is an 11-year-old girl with Asperger Syndrome. At home, all Cindy can think or talk about is the television show *I Love Lucy*. She is obsessed with this program. In her bedroom, she plays with her dolls and pretends that each one is a character from the *I Love Lucy* show. She knows the entire history of the program and remembers every single episode.

In school, all she talks about is *I Love Lucy*. Her classmates are frustrated by her limited interests and constantly tell her to get lost. One day Cindy goes to see her therapist and explains that no one will play with her. Her therapist quickly deduces her underlying problem and tells her that she needs to be willing to talk about other people's interests too. Cindy has trouble understanding this concept, but agrees to try it.

The next day, everyone at school is talking about the television show, *American Idol*. Cindy has never seen this show before and has no real interest in it. In fact, she has never even heard of it. As she sits down with a group of girls, she has no idea what they are talking about. Trying to take the advice of her therapist, she enters the conversation by disingenuously saying, "I love that show."

Her classmate replies, "Really? Who do you think will get voted off tomorrow night?"

Not knowing what to say, Cindy says, "Voted off, what do you mean?"

The whole group of girls looks at her in total bewilderment. "I thought you said you loved that show. You don't even know what 'voted off' means?"

Cindy is clearly embarrassed in not only being caught in a lie, but also being exposed as having nothing in common with her peers.

Lack of imagination

It is important to point out that many individuals with Asperger's have incredible imaginations. Many of the greatest thinkers of all time have been suspected of having Asperger Syndrome, and books have been devoted to that topic. Still, Baron-Cohen and Craig (1999) point out that many children with ASD lack imagination. In fact, this characteristic is one of the diagnostic criteria for being diagnosed with autism. This characteristic isn't as pronounced in Asperger's, but can certainly manifest itself in various ways.

For example, it is generally observed that people with Asperger's don't like to lie. Lying requires a certain amount of imagination because the lie itself is not based upon reality. Lack of imagination can also manifest itself in experiencing difficulty with issues of pretend play in childhood. Most play involves using one's imagination. For example, many childhood games require role playing, like "cops and robbers." This type of activity could pose a problem for someone with Asperger's.

One of my friends is an autism consultant. She explained to me that one of her clients, an 11-year-old boy with Asperger's, had a difficult time playing "hide and seek" with her. The boy insisted that my friend, the consultant, always hide in the same spot so he would know exactly where to find her. My friend had trouble explaining to him that "hide and seek" is not fun if you always know where the person is going to hide. Again, because he lacked imagination (and was rigid), it was hard for him to engage in appropriate play for an 11-year-old. Another 12-year-old with Asperger's, Peter, demonstrates this characteristic.

Though Peter tries hard and wants to be liked by his peers, he often has a difficult time gaining their acceptance. This is due, in part, to his pathological honesty. One day, a student in Peter's class put a whoopee cushion under the teacher's chair. The teacher was furious when, after she sat down, a cacophony of laugher erupted among the students. "If the culprit does not come forward, the whole class will be punished," the teacher shouted.

Peter saw who did it. Without hesitation, he shouted, "It was Barry!" The whole class looked at Peter as if he had just broken the biggest unwritten rule of all time.

"Barry, I want you to take your books and go down to see Mr. Phillips in the principal's office. Thank you, Peter. You are such a helpful student. Class, if all of you could be more like Peter, the world would be a better place."

Later that day, Barry and several of his friends caught up with Peter in the playground. "You're dead, you hear me? You shouldn't have even thought of coming to school today, you snitch, I'm going to beat the crap out of you! Meet me by the flagpole after school!"

Odd use of language

Many individuals with Asperger's are known for sounding like "little professors" in that their use of speech is highly precocious for their age (Attwood 1998). They may even be hyperlexic in that their vocabulary may be huge, but using those words in their appropriate context may prove difficult. It should also be noted that individuals with Asperger's take a highly concrete and literal approach to expressing and understanding language. Phrases like "I am spent" (meaning I'm tired) or "she talked my ear off" might be confusing to the person with Asperger's. Indeed, both the literal interpretation and the pragmatic expressive aspects of language could easily set someone up as being a target for being bullied. Take the following monologue that a ten-year-old boy with Asperger's might say to someone:

> You know, I was just remarking to my father how intrinsically pristine the flowers in our garden are today. My mother is an expert gardener and loves flowers. I love flowers too. They have such a wonder and a beauty about them. They majestically make me very happy.

There are several things to note about this monologue. First, even though the boy chose some sophisticated words, a couple of them were used inappropriately. The words "intrinsically" and "majestically" simply don't make sense in the context of each sentence, even though they are highly advanced words for a ten-year-old. Also, this boy is speaking in such a formal and pedantic way that it clearly would isolate him from his peers. Can you imagine how a fellow ten-year-old would react to those statements? He or she would probably walk away, or start teasing this boy. Either way, odd use of language sets up these children for being targets of bullying.

Summary points

The following attributes associated with Asperger's make it more likely that the person will end up being a target for bullies.

- *Low frustration tolerance* results in a decreased ability to function in one's environment. Frustration tolerance is exacerbated by an inability to deal with sensory stimuli, perfectionism, and unpredictability. When frustration increases and reaches a threshold, it can lead to a meltdown, which makes the person stand out as being different.

- *Monotropism* makes it difficult for individuals to pay attention to more than one piece of information at a time. This can cause someone to miss important pieces of information and stay "stuck" during a conversation and can have an adverse effect on one's social skills.
- *Motor difficulties* result in a decreased ability to perform academic tasks involving writing and drawing. They also make physical education class very challenging. Difficulty with motor issues easily shows up in the playground and in the classroom.
- *Gullibility* causes a person to believe everything he or she hears, therefore being set up to be the butt of a joke.
- *Auditory processing difficulties* result in slow processing of auditory information that makes it hard to formulate a quick comeback.
- *Problems with reading non-verbal cues* make it difficult to read body language and can cause misinterpretation of information from one's peers. Not understanding what seems obvious to everyone else may frustrate peers.
- *Special interests* may seem out of the norm, and other students may find those interests boring.
- *Lack of experience* in the dating arena may be perceived as someone being gay.
- *Cultural illiteracy* becomes a problem because most conversations in adolescence revolve around the popular culture. People with Asperger's may get teased for not knowing about certain topical information.
- *Lack of imagination* creates a problem in playing games that involve pretending. Also, it causes inappropriate responses when telling the truth is not the best option in a social situation.
- *Odd use of language* will often sound like a "little professor" talking. This makes it hard to relate to others at age-appropriate levels.

Chapter 3

Empowering Victims

The previous chapter analyzed various reasons why children with Asperger Syndrome often present themselves as easy targets for bullying and victimization. This chapter will explore specific ways that these victims can be empowered to deal more effectively with bullies and to process the resulting negative experiences.

The powerlessness of victims

Victims of bullying are powerless because, in general, they have very little control over their lives. Just as children who are abused by their parents can't move out of their homes without a court order, children who are being bullied can't transfer schools on their own volition. Even if they could, it is likely they would just encounter bullying at another school. In fact, some research suggests that this population, more than any other group, has fewer choices about their own surroundings, with the exception of prison inmates (Dziuba-Leatherman and Finkelhor 1994). Children who are bullied lack the freedom to leave school or to take action that will change their situation. In a sense, they are prisoners of their surroundings with no escape in sight.

Children with Asperger Syndrome have fewer choices than the average child who is bullied because they lack the skills necessary to respond to being victimized. Not knowing how to act when confronted by a bully, or even being able to recognize when such a situation occurs, drastically impairs one's ability to make appropriate choices. For example, if my boss is abusing me but I don't have that awareness, I probably won't leave my job. If someone is in an abusive marriage and he or she doesn't recognize that it's abusive, that person is not likely to leave the marriage or even seek counseling.

To make choices in our lives, we need to be able to know when we are being victimized. Without that recognition, it is almost impossible to take action.

Children with Asperger Syndrome often are not aware when they are being bullied. Parents frequently share their frustration with me about their children not communicating with them about being bullied at school. In all probability, the children themselves don't know they're being bullied.

The recognition of bullying, therefore, is an educational issue. Victim awareness has to become part of the Individualized Educational Plan (IEP) so that when bullying occurs, a child has the skills to recognize what is happening.

Although some children aren't exactly aware that they're being victimized, they usually know something bad is happening to them. Intuitively, they have figured out that they are different. Their self-esteem has probably been lowered due to repeated victimization. In other words, even though the totality of being victimized on a daily basis has had a negative cumulative effect, it may still be difficult for the child to discern on a case-by-case basis when bullying is taking place. This lack of awareness exacerbates the powerlessness of the victim. It would be like having physical symptoms but not knowing what is causing the ailment. For example, if I am having symptoms of mononucleosis (glandular fever) but I don't have a diagnosis, I won't know how to treat my symptoms. I may be suffering from low energy and fatigue, but without a diagnosis, I may conclude that my physical problems are psychosomatic or "all in my head." If I am not advised to get rest and avoid strenuous activity, the effects of my illness will only get worse. In the same way, if children with Asperger's do not know they are being bullied, they won't know how to combat it effectively and the effects will only worsen.

In the last chapter, I talked about my special interest as a child in interstate expressways. At times, other children would tease me about this interest, but I processed their reactions incorrectly and thought they admired me. They would ask me to tell them where a certain interstate highway began and ended. I misinterpreted those questions as showing interest, rather than making fun of me. As an adult, I can now reflect back and realize that these classmates wanted to expose how odd I was by repeatedly trying to get me to talk about my "weird interest." Because I have Asperger's, it was very difficult for me to be able to read the social intentions of my peers.

Make bullying recognition part of the IEP

In the United States, an Individualized Education Plan exists for special education students to help them succeed at school and is entered into between the school and a child's parent(s). It is designed to target individual weaknesses (thus being deficit-driven as opposed to being strength-based) by creating annual goals and short-term objectives meant to improve upon these weaknesses. One of the frustrating aspects about IEPs is that they primarily focus on what a student cannot do, rather than building on the student's strengths.

However, an IEP is useful in outlining several guidelines for services and accommodations for a student who needs them to succeed. Most of these accommodations consist of having extended time on tests, using calculators, computers or scribes, and participating in occupational therapy. Much of the focus is strictly on academics and core coursework. But for a student with Asperger Syndrome, the focus should also include incorporating the development of social goals into the curriculum. One of the social goals that should be addressed is recognizing when a bullying attempt is being made and what to do when it happens. Heinrichs (2003) suggests that a child's recognition of this fact (or the lack thereof) should be placed in the Present Levels of Educational Performance (PLEP) section of the IEP. The PLEP quantitatively and qualitatively gives information as to a student's present level of performance in a given area. An example of a statement in the PLEP would be "Martin reacts to bullying by crying at least twice a day."

It might be stated in the PLEP that Martin rarely reports bullying when it happens. It might also be reported that 80 percent of classmates interviewed in a self-report measure said they do not like spending time with him. Using Heinrichs' example, an annual goal for Martin might be to develop and maintain an interpersonal relationship with at least one person in the class (Heinrichs 2003). A short-term goal could be that Martin tries to gain more popularity or acceptance (in self-report measures) by a certain date.

However, Heinrichs warns that one of the dangers of creating an IEP in this manner is that it might convey to the child that it's his or her fault if he or she is bullied and, if only the child would change, the bullying would decrease. Read the following objective in this hypothetical IEP and decide if there is an implied sense of judgment: "Billy will gain 50 percent more affirmative answers in the next self-report measure when children are asked if they enjoy spending time with him."

A reasonable interpretation of this objective implies that it is Billy who needs to change in order to be more accepted by his peers. I believe such an objective is unrealistic and could set Billy up for failure. It is much more important to teach Billy to identify when he is bullied rather than trying to assess his development based on whether or not his peers like him. Building inclusiveness should be the goal of a school, not the responsibility of each child. When tackling the problem from a macrocosmic level, it puts the responsibility on the school and the teachers to promote acceptance of a given child by other students. A far better annual goal would be: Billy will learn the skills necessary to be able to recognize bullying and report it when it happens.

This goal doesn't require Billy to alter his personality in any way. It does, however, teach Billy the skills he needs to have when someone is acting in a predatory manner towards him. In Chapter 7, parents will learn ways in which they can help empower their Asperger children to recognize the difference between playful teasing and vicious bullying.

To tell or not to tell

I cannot count the number of times I have been asked (or heard others asked) whether or not parents should tell their child that he or she has Asperger Syndrome. I will give my opinion in a moment, but first I want to address how this is relevant to empowering victims.

Tim and Ted are children with Asperger Syndrome, both 14 years old. They don't know each other, but they live only a few miles apart. They were both diagnosed with Asperger's at age 12 and are often bullied at school. The main difference between them is that Tim's parents have decided not to tell him he has Asperger's while Ted's parents have told him. Every day when Tim is bullied, he internalizes it and blames himself. He knows something is different about him but he can't put his finger on it. This sense of always wondering why he is different creates depression. Ted is also depressed. His parents told him that he has Asperger Syndrome and he thinks it's a death sentence. He rationalizes that others bully him because he has a "disease" that makes him repellent to other people.

Playing devil's advocate, I have given two entirely different arguments why it is not good either to withhold a diagnosis or to disclose it. In my professional life, I have met practitioners who strongly advocate for disclosure as well as those who are vehemently against it. One can argue reasonably either way. Withholding the diagnosis can cause much confusion and turmoil. When episodes of bullying take place, Asperger children know they are different but the lack of any real understanding can create a negative self-image. On the other hand, sharing the diagnosis may label the child as "defective," and he or she could become even more depressed after receiving that information.

Asperger Syndrome is nothing to be ashamed of. It is not a death sentence, nor is it a character defect. The fact is that Asperger Syndrome is a neurobiological difference. It results in perceiving the world through a slightly different lens than others. Many people have speculated that Thomas Jefferson and other notable geniuses may have had Asperger's. There is no shortage of brilliance among the population (Ledgin 2002). Along with this brilliance and uniqueness come differences from the general population. Unfortunately, those who have differences (or stick out in a crowd) are usually the ones who suffer the most from peer abuse while growing up.

Of course not everyone with Asperger Syndrome is a genius, but most people with Asperger's who I've met have some kind of unique personality traits, interests, or talents. Gail Hawkins (2004) states that these unique qualities have led to some of the greatest contributions to society. Gillberg (2002), a noted author on autism, agrees that people with Asperger Syndrome are a tremendous asset to the world. And yet, these same individuals are the ones who often suffer the most peer abuse in childhood, simply because they are different.

Children have a right to know that their differences actually have a name. The name does not define their entire being but it does serve to provide some additional information for self-knowledge. While many children resist being diagnosed and may not even want to talk about it, these same children could continue to suffer from confusion and depression simply because they don't understand that their differences come from a group of traits that they were born with.

If parents withhold the diagnosis from their child, they should expect that eventually their child will discover this truth later in life. People generally need to acquire self-understanding in order to gain greater self-acceptance. The diagnosis of Asperger's can be the information that helps to accomplish this objective. If a child is not told about this diagnosis, a reasonable assumption the person can make when learning of the diagnosis later in life is that there is something wrong with having Asperger's. For example, if I was diagnosed at age 12 but didn't learn about my diagnosis until adulthood, I would wonder why my parents withheld this information from me. Was there something bad about having Asperger Syndrome that my parents didn't want me to know?

By disclosing the diagnosis to your child, you are letting him or her know that Asperger's is nothing to be ashamed of. You are taking away the confusion and pain of not knowing the answer to the age-old question, "Why me?" Instead, you are empowering your child with the knowledge that being a little different could be the greatest gift the Asperger child can have. As my friend Michael John Carley, president of the Global and Regional Asperger Syndrome Partnership (GRASP), has stated, even if he were given the option to become a neurotypical, he would refuse to take it. He likes being different.

Find role models

One of the best ways to empower people with Asperger's is to find an accomplished adult on the spectrum to be a mentor. When I first received my diagnosis at 27, I had never met anyone who had Asperger's. I had no one with whom to compare myself. Then I attended my first autism conference in Nashville, Tennessee, which gave me an opportunity to meet many highly intelligent and creative individuals with Asperger Syndrome. I was amazed. They were friendly, articulate, successful, and very interesting people with good senses of humor. After having just received my diagnosis, it gave me a great deal of hope during a vulnerable time.

A role model can be extremely worthwhile in helping your child process his or her experiences of being bullied. A role model can genuinely empathize because the role model will have received his or her fair share of bullying. Having a role model would allow the individual with Asperger's to meet a successful adult who went down a similar road, albeit with some battle scars, and came out alive and well at the other end.

Restructured settings

Gray (2003) recommends the use and practice of restructuring settings to avoid bullying confrontations. I have mentioned that many children with Asperger's are hypersensitive to stimuli, which can result in meltdowns in school and make them appear different. I gave the example of a child physically reacting to the noise of a fire alarm during a drill, attracting the attention of bullies. If a teacher knows in advance that this behavior might be stimulated by the loud noise, the teacher could advise the student to bring a pair of earphones or headphones to school that day to cover his or her ears. This plan, while increasing the student's self-advocacy skills, would also reduce the likelihood that the child would show any kind of unusual behavior that could provoke bullying from others.

If the cafeteria is noisy, staff could encourage a buddy to eat lunch with the child away from the lunchroom. The Asperger child may be disoriented by all of the loud noise in the cafeteria, which might make him or her more vulnerable to attacks of bullying. If the child needs a few more minutes to transition between classes, this accomodation should be allowed and even written into the special services section of the IEP.

Suppose Ricky, a boy with Asperger's, has only four minutes between classes to grab his books, go to the bathroom, take his medication, and proceed to the opposite side of a large school for his next class. This might be an incredibly difficult task for him due to the amount of multitasking involved. By the time he arrives for class, he's exhausted and anxious to the point where other students will be able to sense his vulnerabilities.

He then gets called on by the teacher and can't properly reply because he's so relieved just to have made it to class on time that he can't focus on anything else. This scenario could provoke teasing by the other students.

Ann Palmer (2006), mother of a child with an autism spectrum disorder, used to request that her son's locker be placed near a supportive teacher's classroom. In retrospect, I think that Ms. Palmer's idea would have been very helpful for me as a student. Another idea could be assigning a peer buddy who helps the Asperger child in transitioning from one class-room to another. If Ricky was having trouble getting ready for each class, the peer buddy could say, "Hey Ricky, time to load up your pencils and put away your books." It would be wise to have these accommodations written into the IEP.

A safe haven

As previously mentioned, a meltdown is an invitation for bullies to identify their prey. Meltdowns signal a complete loss of control and occur when a person is so overwhelmed by the environment that he or she is unable to provide any resistance when being attacked. Therefore, it is imperative that a school setting not create any kind of situation where the possibility of a meltdown is increased for a child with Asperger's.

It is critical for a part of an IEP to provide a safe room where a child with Asperger's can go when he or she feels a meltdown is about to occur.

This is a logical and reasonable request. Think about it. If you are about to throw up, you would head for nearest sink or toilet. You wouldn't just stand there and vomit all over the floor in front of other people. Children need a safe place at school where they can go when they feel a meltdown is imminent. Teaching children to go to this room helps them to exercise self-control and practice their skills in metacognition, which is the ability to monitor their own thoughts. It is far better to be able to sense a meltdown is coming than to have it occur unexpectedly in the wrong place. Even adults with Asperger Syndrome need safe havens at times. I have attended conferences where there is a clearly designated room for people with Asperger's to go if they begin to feel overwhelmed. One conference called it a "chill room."

Many teachers use time-out rooms as punishment for students, a technique I don't especially care for. However, time-out rooms should be clearly differentiated from safe havens. Safe havens should not be used as a punishment or a reward. Their purpose is to help prevent meltdowns and to comfort those who may be on the verge of one.

False victims

Research suggests that there is a state of mind, known as the false victim mentality (Besag 1989; Perry, Perry, and Kusel 1988), which occurs when a person always feels like a victim, irrespective of circumstances. At school, this would translate to someone complaining all the time to staff about being teased or bullied, even when that was not the case.

There is evidence that children with Asperger Syndrome have the potential to fall into this category for a couple of reasons. First, they feel much more comfortable around adults than children their own age because adults are more mature and less likely to abuse them. This fact is well established in the general literature. As a result of feeling uncomfortable around children and more comfortable around adults, a child with Asperger's might try to convince the teacher that someone is bullying him or her. In this way, the child would be able to elicit the attention and sympathy of an adult while rationalizing the need to remain distant from his or her peers.

The second and perhaps more compelling reason is that children with Asperger's often have trouble distinguishing good-natured kidding from bullying. Literalness and an inability to understand sophisticated nuances or jokes can cause innocent behavior to be misconstrued as intended to be hurtful. Therefore, attempts to joke around may be viewed by the child with Asperger's as attempts to bully. Teachers and parents should be aware of this possible tendency. In Chapter 7 on empowering parents, the young person with Asperger's will be given strategies that will help to discern between a playful and a vicious tease.

Provocative victims

Boulton and Smith (1994) coined the term "provocative victim" as someone who *unintentionally* provokes others (in an aggressive way) which then leads to that person being bullied.

Many children with Asperger Syndrome can be brutally honest (Wing 2001). "Joe's stupid, so I won't work with him" could be a comment that a child with Asperger's might make. These types of comments are highly provocative and can invite criticism and anger. To avoid such situations, it's a good idea to devise a strategy to be included in the IEP about this type of unwitting aggressive behavior. For this youngster, it would be imperative that he learns not to talk badly about people in front of them. This is a simple, concrete, and easy-to-follow rule that can help keep someone with Asperger's out of trouble.

Catastrophizing and thought stopping

Children with Asperger Syndrome often lack mental flexibility (Ozonoff and Griffith 2000). As mentioned earlier, their difficulties with executive function (planning, organizing, strategizing) make it hard for them to multitask. Lack of central coherence can make it extremely challenging to generate a broader meaning out of many small details. So, what does all this mean in plain English?

- If you have trouble discerning the broader meaning from a bunch of details in social situations, you will most likely miss the "larger picture."

- If you miss the gist of what's going on, you are likely to be in an anticipatory or fearful state, anxious about what will be said next that will cause you to make more social mistakes.

- If you are always in an anxious state, you will be using a lot of your energy during the day worrying about the bad things that are likely to happen to you. Could this explain, in part, the anxiety that Asperger children experience on a daily basis?

Brown *et al.* (1986) point out that catastrophizing about the future can be a habitual response for all individuals from middle childhood through adolescence if they have been the constant recipient of repeated bullying. Helplessness or powerlessness is generally the prevailing feeling while the person is catastrophizing (Seligman 1975).

Wing (2001) suggests that individuals with Asperger's have an uncanny ability to sense negativity in another person. Thus, they will not want to socialize with someone if they sense the other person doesn't like them.

In understanding this information about the anxiety experienced by children with Asperger's on a daily basis, it is reasonable to conclude that they will consistently exhibit anxiety about issues revolving around:

- transitioning
- changes in the environment
- social situations where there is no "script."

It would be logical to assume that children who constantly worry regarding social situations will simply withdraw from them. If they do not learn alternative means of adaptation, other than constantly feeling anxious throughout their school day, they will be more at risk for meltdowns. If they are more at risk for meltdowns, they are also more at risk for being bullied.

Ross (1984) suggests a cognitive technique called *thought stopping* when someone is worrying about future events. His approach involves having the child list all of the potentially pleasurable aspects about an event that he or she is dreading. Another thought-stopping technique is basically to teach the child to say "stop" when negative thoughts start to enter his or her mind (Lazarus and Wolpe 1966). These cognitive approaches are simple exercises designed to help the student calmly reassess the situation.

Sexuality

I have mentioned that many adolescents with Asperger's are viewed by their peers as being gay, due to a lack of dating experience. Also relevant are Henault's (2005) clinical observations that suggest homosexuality in the Asperger population may be overrepresented. For those individuals who are both gay and have Asperger's, the pain and isolation they experience must be considerable. These individuals need to be able to accept all aspects of who they are. Self-acceptance can rarely take place in hostile environments. Teachers and schools must create an atmosphere where prejudice and harassment of homosexuals is completely unacceptable. Many schools have set up gay/straight alliances, which is a good first step. Just as people with Asperger's can be victimized for their differences, so can gay people. It is essential that both of these differences be accepted by authority figures in the school setting.

The social isolation factor

Forming friendships is a major developmental task of childhood (Hartup 1996). Studies have shown that children who are usually bullied are generally those who have few friends (Brooks, Bartini, and Pellegrini 1999). Most children with Asperger's lack a large social support network, meaning they don't have many friends.

When I was in the seventh grade, one of the counselors at school noted that I was socially isolating myself. She called my parents and recommended that I be placed in a social skills group, which at that time was called group therapy. My dad told me that this was a group of kids who were struggling socially, like I was. Based on that description, can you guess if I wanted to join this group? I'll give you a hint: no! I did go to this group once a week for almost a year, but I fought my parents tooth and nail every time I had to go.

Interestingly, I never turned down the opportunity to play tennis with my peers. In fact during the summer, I used to play eight hours of tennis a day with people my age! So, what was the difference between the therapy group and the tennis group? Finding a special interest that I could share with others. In all truthfulness, I was never bullied when I was taking a tennis lesson, which may be another reason I loved playing tennis.

Some children with Asperger's are simply introverted by nature and don't like being very social, while others are extremely social and try to fit in, without much success. I was definitely the former. My social tolerance threshold was low in most situations and high with activities revolving around my special interests.

So what am I saying? It is imperative to find activities for children with Asperger's that involve their special interests. These activities will build self-esteem and self-confidence more than any social skills group. In this day and age, there is virtually a group for every interest imaginable. Sometimes, it just takes a little bit of legwork on the parts of parents and teachers.

How will you know that a child has a special interest? When my father took me to my first baseball practice, I wanted to quit right away. When he wanted me to compete on the swim team, the same thing occurred. But the first day I held a tennis racquet in my hand, I loved it! I never complained about going to play tennis at the local tennis club. So the answer is simple. If a child enjoys the activity and there's no resistance, chances are it's a special interest or at least one worth pursuing.

It is also worth pointing out that successful social interaction does not have to occur with same-aged peers. A well-known fact in the general literature on Asperger Syndrome is that individuals often feel more comfortable with people a lot older or younger than they are. Perhaps if the person with Asperger Syndrome volunteers at a nursing home, he or she could get social stimulation and perhaps feel increased self-esteem. Or maybe the person could help out at an after-school daycare center that would increase his or her leadership capabilities. Let me reiterate that people with Asperger Syndrome often do not do well in traditional social settings. School dances, football games, and after-school activities may not be the places where someone with Asperger's will thrive. Finding unique settings where people with Asperger's can shine or at least feel comfortable should be the overriding goal.

Hygiene

I can remember on several occasions in school, classmates would refer to my poor hygiene. I was teased and often felt humiliated about this lack of self-care. Gillberg (2002) notes that poor hygiene can be a major problem for children and adolescents with Asperger Syndrome. Many of these issues are sensory related. The child may not like the feeling of the toothbrush on the gums, or the loud sound of the hairdryer, or the pressure of the water from the showerhead as it hits the body.

It's understandable that some activities involving daily cleansing might be uncomfortable for someone with Asperger's. However, a major source of teasing and bullying can result from body odor and bad breath, aside from the health risks presented. Therefore, it is important that these issues be addressed. Find the toothbrushes with the softest bristles. See if there are alternative ways of cleaning one's body and washing one's hair, like taking a bath versus taking a shower. Help the child understand the potential health and social consequences of poor hygiene.

The martial arts

For whatever reason, motor clumsiness is a hallmark of Asperger's. Hans Asperger (1944/1991) himself noticed that his patients had significant motor issues. Tantam (1991) stated that 91 percent of the people in his study of 60 Asperger adults exhibited motor clumsiness. With poor motor abilities and difficulties in maintaining balance, individuals with Asperger's are at a true disadvantage in terms of defending themselves. Not only is verbal abuse a consequence of becoming a victim of bullying, but so is physical violence.

I recommend that every child with Asperger's be exposed to some martial arts training. Not only would it give them a sense of learning about their own bodies, but it can also increase one's ability to engage in self-defense when necessary to do so.

Share the good news

When I was in middle school, I thought that people were always going to be mean to me for the rest of my life. Back then I guess you could say I was a misanthrope. My thinking was that people would be cruel to me through-out my entire life. At the time, I knew some 80-year-olds who were nice to me, but I thought that was just because I was a child. I thought when I turn 80, everyone will still be as mean to me as they are today.

Of course, as adults, we know this gloomy outlook isn't true. Most people do get nicer as they get older. Most adults do not get joy out of tor-menting other adults. This isn't to say that bullying and victimization doesn't happen in adulthood, but certainly not to the same degree.

I wish I could have understood when I was 12 that eventually as I got older people were going to be nicer to me. Maybe then I wouldn't have gone through middle school thinking people were going to be cruel to me for the rest of my life. I would have had a light at the end of the tunnel.

Encourage opportunities for leadership

Generally speaking, people who are seen as leaders aren't bullied. They are admired and respected. There might have been a time where it was thought that people with autism or Asperger Syndrome couldn't assume leadership roles, but those days are gone.

Individuals with Asperger Syndrome can thrive in various leadership roles, given the right circumstances. My first cousin, Arthur, who also has Asperger Syndrome and is in his thirties, is a prime example. As a child, he wasn't very outgoing because he was bullied throughout his adolescence at school. One summer, he went to a camp in the Catskills area of New York where he became immersed in the Jewish religion and the culinary arts. It was at this camp that he discovered two of his special interests: cooking and Judaism. He is now a chef at one of the best restaurants in the Metro Detroit area.

About ten years ago, Arthur was also able to take his interest in religion and assume a leadership role at his temple, which has one of the largest Jewish congregations in the United States. He is now the head usher at services, in charge of Homeless Week, and serves on the board of directors. Recently, he was named Man of the Year and a dinner was given to honor him with over 300 people in attendance.

Maybe Arthur always had this leadership potential inside of him but was not able to tap into it until adulthood. I often wonder: would he have been bullied as a child if an adult had given him the opportunity to tap into his leadership potential earlier? I don't think so.

Recently I gave a speech at a high school to a group of students with Asperger Syndrome. As I entered the classroom, one young man approached me, introduced himself and said, "I can't stay very long. I have to get ready for the prom." The teacher told me later that this student was captain of the football team and one of the most beloved students at his school. Another student who I met ran successfully for student congress. Recently in the news, there was a young man with autism from upstate New York who made headlines by sinking six three-point baskets in a row within the last minutes of a high-school basketball game, helping his team make it to the state finals. He had already established himself as a leader on the team as the coach's helper and water boy long before he put on a uniform and stepped on the court. Once given the opportunity, he became the hero of his team.

People with Asperger Syndrome are interesting and capable people who can thrive when provided with leadership roles. Ideally, good leaders:

- are dependable
- keep their word
- stand up for what they believe and do not just conform to others
- stay focused and determined
- are sincere and genuine.

All of these leadership traits are usually shared by people with Asperger's.

Consider homeschooling

Homeschooling is certainly not right for everyone and isn't a decision that should be taken lightly. But when all else fails, it can be a practical alternative to the daily torture and abuse that someone with Asperger's may suffer at school. Parents who consider homeschooling have probably tried every other alternative, since it involves such a major time commitment on the parents' part.

A parent should consider homeschooling their child if:

- the child is frequently in physical danger at school and the school seems ill equipped to handle the problem
- the child has tried various schools without success

- continuing to attend school compromises the child's mental health
- moving districts or locations is out of the question
- parents have the time, educational background, and resources to organize and implement a homeschool program.

The worry I hear parents most often express about homeschooling is that their child will not have the same opportunities for socialization as their school-aged peers. If socialization means being bullied and humiliated on a daily basis, so be it! It is very hard to perform well academically when one's energy is focused on merely getting through the day.

If parents take the time to facilitate outside activities around the child's interests, he or she can still gain valuable social experience. Just because a person may be gaining his or her experience socializing in unconventional ways, this doesn't make that experience any less valuable. Remember, people with Asperger Syndrome are unconventional people!

Make certain provisions

It has been stressed that adults should do everything they can so that children with Asperger's can avoid having meltdowns. However, sometimes meltdowns are unavoidable. When they do happen, teachers need to possess the knowledge and expertise to take into consideration environmental stressors, including being bullied, which are likely to be part of the equation. Heinrichs (2003) talks about the fact that many children who are bullied chronically will react in drastic ways. Children with Asperger Syndrome may sometimes go to extreme measures to defend themselves when pushed to the limit.

Zero-tolerance policies can sometimes cause harsh results for individuals with Asperger's who take inappropriate action in order to defend themselves. I recommend that it be written into the IEP that the child who overreacts be viewed in the context of all surrounding circumstances rather than on the sole basis of his or her isolated actions.

Summary points

- The prison population is the only group with less freedom than children who are regularly bullied.
- Children with Asperger Syndrome do not always realize when they are victims of bullying.

- Not knowing when they are being bullied puts children in a powerless situation.
- The PLEP section of an IEP should indicate the present level of performance as it relates to a student's ability to discriminate when he or she is being bullied.
- Annual goals and short-term objectives should help the student gain this recognition.
- Children need to have Asperger Syndrome explained to them in such a way that it helps to increase, not decrease, their self-esteem.
- Adult role models who have Asperger Syndrome can help children understand that they are not alone in being bullied.
- Restructuring school settings can help children avoid meltdowns, and thereby reduce chances for bullying.
- Students with Asperger Syndrome need a safe haven in the school where they can go when they feel a meltdown coming on.
- To gain the attention of adults, some children with Asperger's might act like "false victims."
- Sometimes children with Asperger's can unintentionally provoke people into bullying them.
- It helps students with Asperger's to cognitively "stop thinking" when they find themselves catastrophizing about future events.
- Students with Asperger Syndrome who are gay need just as much acceptance and support as heterosexual students.
- Encourage the child to become involved in social activities around areas of special interest.
- Find ways to improve hygiene, as bad hygiene often leads to teasing.
- Encourage the child to participate in the martial arts.
- Encourage opportunities for leadership.
- Consider homeschooling if all other options have failed.
- Make certain provisions for understanding extreme behavior taken for self-protective reasons.

Chapter 4

Empowering Bystanders

One of the things that struck me in researching bullying prevention is the crucial role of the bystander. Almost every article or book that I read focused considerable attention on the role of the bystander. In terms of my own victimization, I can see how bystander apathy contributed to my having been bullied so frequently throughout the years.

There were many times when I was growing up when I felt hopeless. Reflecting on those times, I can think of what would have been the most helpful to me:

- if a bystander had said to the person bullying me, "Leave him alone"
- if a bystander had publicly condemned the bully's behavior and then invited me to sit at his or her table at lunch
- if several bystanders had come to my aid and befriended me.

Sadly, these aforementioned scenarios rarely occurred. Rather, I was always at the mercy of bullies because I had no supporters coming to my defense. Apparently, no one felt moved enough to stand up for me. That inaction or apathy triggered internalized feelings of worthlessness and shame. The bystanders' failure to show support for me essentially communicated to me that they felt I deserved the kind of treatment I was receiving at the hands of the bullies.

In this chapter, the bystander's role in bullying will be explored along with the concept of how crucial bystander intervention is in curbing the bullying problem.

One way to take action and prevent bullying is to get everyone involved, particularly bystanders. This course of action is consistent with the belief that most people possess good character and want to help others in need.

Most responsible human beings will report injustice if they see it. If a person observes a mother beating her child, that witness is likely to report this incident to Child Protective Services. Strangely enough, this same kind of protective action is rarely taken with bullying in schools. There is an inherent secret code of silence that neurotypicals learn very early in life (Heinrichs 2003). The code of silence goes something like this: *It doesn't matter what you saw; don't tell!*

Consider how harmful this type of socialization message is and the pain it causes victims of bullying. If an adult beat up another adult, criminal charges would be brought, but if a child beats up another child, he or she is likely to suffer no consequences or at most get a detention or be suspended. Something is definitely wrong here. Why shouldn't an assault be considered an assault, regardless of a person's age?

This chapter strongly advocates that the most important intervention for the bystander is getting involved. Schools must try to create a culture where children learn to stick up for each other and if one child sees another in trouble, the natural inclination would be to support that student. Instead of looking at bystander involvement as tattling, it should be regarded as an act of caring. The rationale for bystander involvement is that bullying is an antisocial act and is wrong.

What is bullying?

We will return to the concept of bystanders, but first we need some clarity about how bullying should be defined.

For bullying to occur, there must be an imbalance of power, an attempt to assert that power over another individual, an intent to harm, and a threat of further aggression—usually covert and not something actually said out loud (Coloroso 2003).

Coloroso then goes on to say that, if left untreated, a fifth element is added: *terror!*

Let's analyze each of these factors through the characters Joe Cool and Bill Geek.

Imbalance of power

To create or enhance an imbalance of power, one person benefits from a base of support. The stronger the base of support, the greater the potential for an imbalance of power. If Joe Cool wants to bully Bill Geek, he will be less successful if others don't support him. Joe's "base of support" are the bystanders in the area. If the bystanders do not intervene and tell Joe that bullying isn't cool, then Joe will be more likely to continue bullying Bill. The bottom line is that one cannot assert power over another person if there is not a power imbalance, and there is a greater likelihood for a power imbalance to occur when the bully receives peer support. Eighty-five percent of bullying takes place within the presence of other children (Coloroso 2003). This fact clearly indicates that bullying is a social activity and doesn't usually occur in a vacuum.

Exploiting weaknesses

Out of this imbalance of power comes the urge to exploit the weakness of others. Once Joe Cool sees that he has a power imbalance over Bill Geek, he's going to want to exercise that power. It is like depositing money into a bank account. The more money one has, the more likely a person is going to be tempted to spend that money. The less money one has, the more frugal a person will be.

Intent to harm

Once it is established that a person has power over someone else and the ability to exercise that power, the next step would be to hurt that person. In other words, a true power imbalance means having the ability to hurt another person either physically, emotionally, or both. In harming another individual, the power imbalance actually manifests itself.

Threat of further aggression

Once the bully sees that he or she has the power to hurt another person, the bully likes that feeling and it may increase his or her self-esteem. The bully doesn't want to lose the feeling of power, so he or she lets the victim know that there is more abuse to come.

The basic emotion experienced by the victim of bullying is terror. The victim is never quite sure where and when he or she is going to be targeted. Over time, a feeling of paranoia begins to engulf the victim.

Terror magnified for the person with Asperger's

This terror would be even greater for an individual with Asperger Syndrome for the following reasons.

- Individuals with Asperger Syndrome have difficulty tolerating transitions or surprises. Being bullied usually comes as a surprise as bullies tend to strike without warning. This type of surprise attack would be an extra jolt to the nervous system of someone with Asperger's.

- William Stillman (2006) states that individuals with Asperger's are exquisitely sensitive human beings. This means that there would not be as strong a protective emotional shield around people with Asperger's as there would be for the neurotypical population. Thus, each incident of bullying would be cumulatively more draining, exhausting, and frightening.

- Individuals with Asperger's tend to be black-and-white thinkers, which means that they may think the worst, even if another person was merely being playful with them. (More about this in Chapter 7.)

Coloroso (2003) eloquently states that once terror is created, the bully can act without any fear of consequences of retaliation. Therefore, disciplinary action taken by the school against the bully will not be nearly as effective as the disapproval or action taken by peers. As established earlier, one of the reasons an imbalance of power exists is because other children condone the act of bullying. Without the support (or even the apathy) of the bystanders, the bully loses all incentive. Why would someone want to bully another child if the act of bullying itself wasn't going to bring social rewards? The self-esteem of the bully would not be boosted without the support of others. Hence, under these circumstances, the bully is emasculated.

The focus of the rest of this chapter is to understand ways that bystanders can participate in support of the bully's victim, and ways to rally bystander support.

Bystander intervention

Heinrichs (2003) suggests that bystander intervention can be extremely effective, but it does not happen often. Usually when a bystander intervenes, he or she does so without group support. Most bystanders do not want to risk their social standing by sticking up for an unpopular child. Many people fear that if they came to the aid of the victim, other children would assume a friendship exists with the victim. Therefore, bystander intervention is a very risky business.

If there were a group mindset among children at school that viewed bullying as a socially unacceptable behavior, there would be little incentive to bully. Unfortunately, that kind of mindset does not exist in most schools. How do we go about creating it?

Types of bystanders

Coloroso (2003) identified five different types of bystanders:

1. Follower henchman—takes an active role in bullying but does not start it.

2. Supporter/passive bully—supports the bullying but does not take an active part, i.e. will laugh and cheer but stays primarily on the sidelines.

3. Passive supporter/possible bully—likes the bullying but does not openly display support.

4. Disengaged onlooker—does not take a stand either way and is truly apathetic to the situation.

5. Possible defender—dislikes the bullying and thinks he or she ought to help but fails to do so.

Then there are the actual *defenders* who are few and far between. What is interesting to note is most children fall into the "possible defender" category, meaning they do not like to witness bullying. This means that most students dislike bullying and think they ought to help, but don't act according to their own moral compass. Carol Gray (2003) cites that 84 out of 100 children are empathetic to children being bullied, and yet those same boys and girls are not likely to act as defenders. In fact, Craig and Pepler (1995) conducted a study that further confirmed Gray's findings. Here's what they found.

- Peers (bystanders) were involved in 85 percent of the bullying episodes.

- Peers reinforced the bullying in 81 percent of the episodes.

- Peers were friendlier toward the bullies than their targets. These same peers who often expressed an interest in helping victims and who were specifically trained in antibullying and settling peer disputes often sided with the bullies rather than their victims in managing these disputes.

- Peers intervened in only 13 percent of the episodes when they were present.

These statistics clearly show that most students want to help, but fail to do so. If 84 out of 100 students are empathetic toward the victim and yet most of those same children are "friendlier" toward the bully, something is drastically wrong. How can "possible defenders" be so involved in promoting bullying while at the same time feeling empathy towards the victim? The answer is simple: social pressures!

The problem becomes even more apparent when looking at the child with Asperger Syndrome. As mentioned in Chapter 2, individuals with Asperger's are less likely to enlist bystander support simply because most of them don't have a lot of friends. Consequently, an extreme imbalance arises between the bully and the child with Asperger's due to the increased numbers of bystanders who support the bully or watch apathetically from the sidelines.

This is why I have repeatedly suggested throughout this book that the child with Asperger Syndrome be assigned a buddy to act as a mentor. The mentor system when utilized in schools works extremely well. I have visited several high schools in Michigan where peer-mentoring programs have virtually eliminated bullying of ASD children. With these programs in place, the children with Asperger's are naturally integrated into the mainstream social environment. They are invited to sit with their peers at lunch instead of wandering to the nearest empty table. Their buddy acts as a social aide who can help the child with Asperger's interpret various social cues.

Peer-mentoring programs

Peer mentoring is an excellent way to help integrate ASD students into the mainstream social environment. In schools that use peer-mentoring programs, neurotypical students take a specific class that allows them to become basically familiar with ASD and then they can successfully mentor the ASD child. They receive class credit and can put this experience on their resume. For peer-mentoring programs to be successful, a few prerequisites need to be in place. I recommend the following.

- It should be mandatory that the mentor spend some time outside of school getting to know the person he or she is going to mentor. Social life does not end when the school bell rings at 3:00 p.m. Life goes on and for most people in middle and high school, time outside of school is just as social as during the school day. If a potential buddy refuses to meet this requirement, it is likely that he or she would probably not be a successful mentor. There should be a suggested minimal number of times that the neurotypical mentor spends with his "buddy" outside of school. Ideally, the school should encourage the mentor to include the student in some social activities outside of school so the person with ASD can learn to navigate his way through more complicated social terrain, as opposed to only a one-on-one interaction.

- There should be a minimum time commitment for the mentor to act in that capacity. If a mentor and ASD pupil bond and then in a short time the semester is over, the child with ASD might experience a feeling of great loss. In order for a program like this to truly be effective, the mentor has to make a one- or two-year commitment to his or her mentored pupil.

- The mentor should make a commitment to be available by telephone in case any troublesome issues come up for the ASD child, but the ASD child must agree not to abuse this privilege.

- It would be ideal for peer-mentoring programs to be established for grades 6 through 12. Middle school is notoriously known as being one of the toughest developmental periods, so extra peer support during this time is crucial. An abbreviated version of a peer-mentoring program might be appropriate for the upper grades in elementary school.

- At the end of the semester or year, upon fulfilling a host of other requirements, the students usually receive academic credit for their dutiful mentoring. The mentors would deal primarily with their own issues in the mentoring process rather than disclose what might be confidential information about the ASD child.

Possible defenders

Most children simply do not like bullying. So, then why don't they intervene? Here are a few paraphrased statements from students that provide some rationalizations as to why they remain passive.

- I like the bully.
- I don't care about the victim.
- The victim is such a geek.
- He [the victim] deserved to be bullied.
- Me, a tattletale? No way!
- I don't want to get picked on myself.
- At least, nobody is picking on me. I'd like to keep it that way.

(Coloroso 2003; Heinrichs 2003)

All of these statements are clearly fear-based. They show the disincentive for anyone to act as a defender, and this is exactly how and why the code of silence continually gets reinforced. A person could lose his or her friends and end up being bullied by the group. Why would anyone intervene on behalf of the victim unless they anticipated support from their peers?

Our goal should be to turn "possible defenders" into actual defenders. A group mindset needs to be created so that when students in the playground see someone being victimized, they will intuitively come to the aid of the victim. For example, if Joe Cool is insulting Bill Geek in the presence of bystanders, an army of bystanders would be willing to confront Joe, head-on. This goal is not unrealistic even though such a scenario rarely happens.

Creating a group mindset

Most schools do not even teach the concept of bystander intervention, yet many schools still have bullying prevention programs. How can a bullying prevention program be effective while not having bystanders as the central focus?

I believe that group teaching is the most effective way for children to understand the concept of "bystanders" and the role they should play. Most children do not know what to do when they see others being bullied. Teaching this concept in a group ensures that everyone is provided with the same information. It also helps to create a group mindset and a culture of caring where cruel behavior isn't tolerated. Thus, a "whole-school approach" is recommended where the concept of bystanders is taught in every classroom and at school assemblies. The following are some terms that I believe every student from third grade on should know.

- *Bystander*—a person who watches an event involving bullying happen. When you see someone being bullied, you automatically become a bystander.

- *Bully*—someone who tries to make another person feel bad, by calling that person names, hitting, punching, or kicking them. In short, causing any physical or mental injuries to a person perceived as having less power.

- *Victim*—the person who is bullied.

When a victim is being hurt, the bystanders should take appropriate action to stop the bully or immediately inform an adult. Rebekah Heinrichs (2003) believes that when bystanders do not act in these situations, they passively accept injustice. Consequently, the bystander becomes a willing co-conspirator with the bully. Perhaps there ought to be consequences for bystanders who don't do the right thing. Depending on the circumstances of a particular school, some possible options might be:

- if bystanders participate in the act of bullying, even if they aren't the instigators, they become responsible parties

- if bystanders merely observe an incident and do nothing else, they bear some responsibility in the matter.

What is important to understand is that *bystander apathy* also contributes to the problem of bullying. An apathetic attitude communicates to both the victim and the bully that the bystander approves of the bully's behavior, whether or not that is actually true. In order to create a caring environment, the right attitudes must be instilled among the students. At West Point Military Academy in Hudson, New York, one of the largest school campuses in the world, the cadets are bound by an honor code. If a student cheated on an exam and another student saw it, the witness would be required to turn in his fellow student even if they were good friends. Similarly, if one lawyer knows of another lawyer's acts of serious professional misconduct, the misconduct must be reported to the authorities. Failure to report becomes an act of misconduct in and of itself (American Bar Association 2006).

What about a student honor code that addresses bullying—an honor code which states that if a person sees an incident of bullying take place, he or she has a duty either to report it to a teacher or to confront the bully? Does this sound radical? Is it any more radical than the honor code at West Point or that adopted by the legal profession? Isn't a student bullying another student just as serious an offense as someone cheating on an exam?

If that honor code did not exist at West Point, it would be a lot easier to cheat and get away with it. The stipulation in the honor code creates a culture where cheating is not tolerated. A rule that sanctioned bystander apathy as immoral would create a similar culture where passively witnessing injustice would also not be tolerated.

If that analogy seems far-fetched, go back to the earlier example of someone watching a mother abuse her child without reporting it to Child Protective Services. Most adults could not passively witness injustice of that magnitude and be able to look at themselves in the mirror. Yet for children, this kind of "looking the other way" is often second nature to them.

Asperger children and bystanders

Many children with Asperger's are often labeled "good cops" in the playground, which frequently gets them into trouble with both staff and other children. It seems as if children with Asperger's naturally act as defenders because they are somewhat immune to the negative social consequences of doing so. They aren't as aware that sticking up for the "unpopular" children breaks a tacit social rule. Being popular is not as much of a priority as it is for many neurotypicals. Therefore, it appears that the skill we need to teach the entire student body may come more naturally to the child with Asperger's.

Another reason Asperger children are inclined to be on the front lines as defenders is because they have a strong sense of social injustice, as reported throughout the general literature on Asperger's. In part, this trait is due to a strong proclivity to want to follow rules because of black-and-white thinking.

However, tattling is different to true peer intervention. The difference is that tattling is done to get someone else in trouble while authentic intervention is undertaken to protect someone. It is important that people with Asperger's understand this difference. A good way to remember the difference is with this distinction: *If you are tattling only to get someone in trouble, it's a bad thing to do. If you are trying to protect someone, telling an adult about it is the right thing to do.*

The invisibility of Asperger's

Children with Asperger's are less likely than their peers to enlist bystander support from others. There are several reasons for this. First, most children with Asperger's have fewer friends due to their social difficulties. Second, Asperger Syndrome is considered to be an invisible disability. In other words, the symptoms displayed by the individual with Asperger's are often "soft signs," meaning that inappropriate behaviors that are displayed may look purposeful. An individual with classic autism or with a more visible impairment would be more likely to be viewed with sympathy because his or her unusual behavior is so obviously unintentional. Here is a hypothetical scenario to illustrate this point.

Pete is an individual with classic autism. At recess, he is in the playground grunting loudly. Darius, the school bully, comes over to Pete and starts to taunt him. "Look everyone, it's Hulk Hogan. Let's hear you grunt, Hulk! Oh, Hulk, I'm so scared."

The teacher is on her way to take Darius to the principal's office but before she has the chance, a crowd of people gathers around him.

"Hey, Darius, what's your problem, man? Leave him alone!"

"Yeah, Darius, what do you think you're doing! Leave the guy alone. He can't help it."

Realistically, this is probably what would happen if a bully decided to pick on someone with classic autism. Everyone would rally around the victim and act as "defenders" as well they should. But if Darius were to pick on our friend Bill Geek, who has Asperger's, would the bystanders act the same way? Probably not. Remember our example from Chapter 2, where Eli made grunting noises because the loud sound of the fire alarm caused his sensory circuits to become overloaded. When Eli was taunted for this behavior, no one stuck up for him because everyone thought Eli was intentionally acting weird.

Because children with Asperger's look "normal" on the surface, their peers expect them to behave "normally." Expectations of others are generally formed during a first impression. It often takes a while for the various oddities of Asperger's to make themselves known, so people with Asperger's are often held to neurotypical standards of behavior. Conversely, when first meeting someone with classic autism, it is immediately obvious that there are visible differences in the observed behavior and others' expectations conform to this difference.

Many children with Asperger's have learned the social skills necessary to project a good first impression. Through social stories, comic strip conversations, and other social skills interventions, they may have learned appropriate scripts for greetings and conversational pleasantries. However, there are no "scripts" when the hypersensitive person's sensory circuits are put on overload. When this happens, others are confused. This person seemed normal one moment, so why is he acting so weird now? What actually happened is that he was able to hide his real self from the public view.

Many times people will ask me, "Nick, how are you able to speak in front of an audience with such poise and still have a social disability?" The reason is because I am able to fool my audience. When I give a speech, I have a script and I follow it to the letter, even though it may appear as if I am being totally spontaneous. When people ask me questions at the end of my talk, they are usually questions I have answered many times before...so again, my answers are fairly well scripted. People can hardly believe that I have Asperger Syndrome after watching me give a speech, but it doesn't change the fact that I do.

Should we disclose the Asperger's to the class?

Many parents struggle with this question. On the one hand, they realize that if their child's classmates understand that he or she has a social disability called Asperger Syndrome, that child will receive more sympathy and get bullied less. On the other hand, parents do not want to embarrass their children by labeling them and possibly creating a stigma against the child as viewed by other children.

Realistically, a child with Asperger's will enlist more bystander support if classmates know that he or she has a bona fide social disability. This does not guarantee that the child will become more popular because of the disclosure. If anything, the disclosure could result in even greater isolation. Instead of being teased and abused, it is possible that the child with ASD will now merely be ignored.

Peer exclusion is a covert form of bullying that happens non-verbally. A person who is repeatedly ignored gets a certain message reinforced, which is: *no one wants to be with you. You are not worthy of friends.* I believe this unspoken message is as psychologically harmful as someone actually saying, "I don't like you."

While a disclosure of Asperger's might reduce teasing, it may also increase the isolation. However, there is a flip side of the coin that is worth examining. It is essential to explain what Asperger's is to other children in a dynamic way. If Asperger's is presented to students as merely a "social disability on the autism spectrum that results in impaired communication," it seems only natural that the ASD student will be further isolated. Although teachers should not lie about Asperger's, many of the positive attributes of the syndrome should also be stressed.

A great resource for understanding the upside of Asperger's is Tony Attwood and Carol Gray's "The Discovery of 'Aspie' Criteria" (1999). Here is how Asperger Syndrome could be explained to a group of fifth-grade students.

People with Asperger Syndrome are truly special individuals. They were born with a different way of seeing the world. Not better...not worse...just different. Someone who has Asperger Syndrome is on the autism spectrum. With Asperger Syndrome, it is possible for someone to focus on something for really long periods of time. Lots of people who do not have Asperger's can't do that, or would have a hard time doing it. Many people think Albert Einstein had Asperger Syndrome. He had to stay focused for a long time before he discovered the theory of relativity. Can anyone tell me why being able to focus on something for a long period of time would be a good thing? (Students throw out reasons.) Very good, class! Also, someone with Asperger Syndrome usually tells the truth in most situations. Lots of people who don't have Asperger's would have trouble being as honest. How many of you think being able to tell the truth most of the time is cool? (Children raise their hands.) I think so too! Sometimes people with Asperger's find certain things to be harder than they would be for other people. For example, loud noises can be difficult to tolerate for someone with Asperger's. When the fire alarm goes off, it may hurt their ears whereas it might not hurt your ears. Also, someone with Asperger's might have a hard time understanding various conversations. This is not because they are dumb! It's because their brains work a little differently than yours! Again, not worse, not better. Just different. Lastly, most people with Asperger Syndrome are highly intelligent! You see class, we are all different and as individuals, we all have challenges to overcome and gifts to share with the world.

If you attempt to disclose that a child has Asperger Syndrome to your class, avoid the following words.

- disability
- disorder
- socially challenged
- disease
- normal (to describe the child with Asperger's as not being normal)
- damaged (as in brain damaged).

Using any of these words is sure to isolate the child with Asperger's. The goal is to integrate the child with Asperger's into the mainstream social environment so he or she can receive bystander support and make friends.

Children with Asperger Syndrome are different. When a teacher describes to a class what Asperger Syndrome means, these differences will have to be explained. Individuals with Asperger's have a different way of seeing the world; a different way of reacting to sensory stimuli and a different way of forming social relationships. Unfortunately, being different is usually frowned upon by other children. Everyone wants to fit in, but if someone is "different" because he or she is talented in some special way, the difference is embraced. For example, one of my classmates from elementary school who was very different from everyone else is now an NBA (National Basketball Association) basketball player. In elementary school, he was a head taller than every other child. He was also much more athletically gifted. Did his size and athletic skill turn him into a social outcast? On the contrary! Everyone thought he was the coolest kid in the school because of his differences.

The objective is not to turn children with Asperger's into the coolest kids in school. That probably won't happen. However, differences can be accepted and even embraced if they are presented in a positive way. Every person has gifts, whether the person has Asperger's or not. The goal of the teacher or parent who discloses their child's Asperger diagnosis is to highlight those gifts and bring them to the forefront.

Find ways to compliment exemplary behavior

As mentioned earlier, doing the ethical act often comes naturally for the person with Asperger Syndrome. In the culture of caring, where the new gold standard is for people to report injustice when they see it, it is important to find ways to compliment the individual with Asperger's who acts according to the high moral ground. In some ways, the person with Asperger's can serve as a role model for the rest of the school in this regard.

There are things that every teacher should *not* do if they are interested in encouraging bystander support.

Don't set up popularity contests

First, any activity that sets up a popularity contest is a huge no-no. I recently talked to a mother of a child with ASD who said her son was crushed because he did not receive any valentine cards from his classmates. I told the woman that I could easily relate to her son's feelings.

Popularity contests are unconsciously engineered by teachers who actually reinforce who is popular and who is not. These contests have the effect of diminishing bystander support for the less popular students. Any activity that has the potential to exclude someone is an activity to be avoided. If a teacher chooses to do a Valentine's Day card exchange, every student should get an equal number. Some teachers may oppose this by saying, "That's not how it works in the real world." True, but if the real world is ever going to function in a way that accepts differences and tolerates diversity, it must begin by teaching children that everyone should be treated equally. If children do not learn that lesson in school, then they certainly won't value that principle when they go out into the real world.

Physical education teachers can also encourage popularity contests by having two captains pick teams. I beg gym teachers not to do that! Many

Asperger children are not athletic at all because they may have poor gross motor skills. Consequently, they will always be picked last. And being picked last in gym class reinforces the fact that they are not popular, which in turn means that when they get bullied, bystanders will be less likely to come to their aid. Again, I can hear gym teachers saying, "That's not how the real world works." The response is that we need to teach children to value the whole person, not just the person who may be more athletic at a particular sport. By having two captains pick teams, you are unwittingly teaching children that it is okay for certain kids to be popular and others to be unpopular based on their athletic skills. There are numerous ways to select teams without being exclusionary. For example, have students count off and the evens and the odds become the teams. It is simply wrong to teach children that athletic children have more human value than those lacking in athletic prowess.

Don't bully the student yourself

If teaching students that bullying is wrong and that bystanders need to report incidents to an authority, a teacher cannot expect to be taken seriously if he or she bullies any student in the classroom. In Chapter 1, teacher bullying was defined as when a teacher uses his or her power as a way of engaging in a purposeful power struggle where the objective is not to help the student, but to harm him or her in some way.

If a teacher tells an ASD student that he or she is "lazy" in front of other students, that statement is an act of bullying. If a teacher tells an ASD child to "try harder" in front of his classmates, again, bullying probably is taking place. Particularly with a child who has Asperger Syndrome, a teacher must be extremely sensitive to what he or she tells the child in front of the child's peers. In Chapter 7, I explain that Asperger children can easily misinterpret behavior as being "mean," even if one's intentions are good. Suppose a child cannot pay attention because there is a humming noise from the fluorescent lights in the room that is distracting him. A teacher says, "Bill, pay attention. I just asked you a question. Can't you ever pay attention? I'm not going to ask you again." Without realizing it, that teacher just condoned the concept of "bullying" to the entire class and made it that much more likely that Bill's classmates will view him in a negative light. As a result, if Bill Geek gets bullied by Joe Cool in the playground, Bill's classmates won't come to his aid. The teacher created a "trickle-down" effect. If the teacher doesn't set a good example, the students will most certainly follow in his or her footsteps.

Communicate with the child's parents

Teachers need to inform parents about how they are helping their child function in the classroom. Let the parent know exactly what is being done to integrate the child with ASD into the mainstream social environment. Inform parents concerning what is being done to curb bullying. Talk about the importance of bystander intervention and what will be done if their child is bullied. A peer-mentoring program would need to be discussed in detail with parents as to how such a program works and the need for the parents' support for such an undertaking. If the parents approve, ask them if they have a preference as to which student mentors would be a good choice to work with their child.

In Chapter 7, I will discuss the reporting by teachers to parents of bullying incidents as they occur. I believe this is essential as it helps to keep the teacher accountable and informs parents about exactly what is happening to their child. Many children with ASD have trouble articulating to their parents the extent to which they have been victimized. As the teacher, you are there to provide the student with a voice. If you are not committed to letting the parents know when and how the ASD child is bullied and what interventions are being employed, then there is no way for those parents to know what is happening to their child while at school. This information is of great importance to parents in better understanding the negative behavior of the child at home that is likely to be related to negative experiences at school or other factors.

Summary points

- Bullying involves an imbalance of power that becomes exacerbated when the bully receives bystander support. Use of that power then leads to a threat of further aggression.
- If bullying is left unchecked, the victim becomes terrorized.
- The ASD child is more susceptible to feeling terrorized for reasons discussed in the chapter.
- Bullies count on bystanders to amplify their imbalance of power.
- Bullying subsides 50 percent of the time when bystanders intervene. This number would probably be higher if a group mindset was established.
- Group teaching creates a group mindset that creates a culture of caring.

- Most children do not like to see bullying, yet they support it directly or indirectly through their inaction or their open support of the bully.

- 84 percent of students are more empathetic to the victim than the bully, but because of peer pressure, they will be more supportive of the bully.

- An honor code should be developed where students must confront the bully or tell someone in authority when they see a person being victimized.

- Many children with Asperger Syndrome naturally act as "defenders" without having to be formally taught, yet they must be taught the difference between tattling and authentic peer intervention.

- The invisibility of Asperger's makes it less likely that a child with that disability will receive bystander support when compared to an individual with a more visible disability.

- If a child with Asperger's discloses his or her diagnosis to the class, it should involve stressing the positives. Remember, the goal is to integrate that student naturally into the mainstream social environment, not to further alienate the child from his or her peers.

- Find ways to compliment exemplary behavior on the part of the child with Asperger's.

- Don't set up popularity contests in your classrooms.

- Don't bully the student yourself.

- Don't play favorites.

- Do a good job communicating with the parents of the ASD child. Explain exactly what you are doing to integrate that student into the mainstream environment and to ensure that the student receives bystander support.

Chapter 5

Empowering Teachers

A few years ago, I learned firsthand how difficult the job of teaching is. At that time, I had set my sights on becoming a special education teacher. My reasoning was that since I had a documented learning disability as a child, this career could be my way of giving something back to people who were growing up as I did. At the time I began my student teaching assignment, I had done extremely well throughout my master's coursework. My grade point average was above a 3.7 (equivalent to an A minus grade: the highest score possible is usually 4.0) and I had no reason to believe that student teaching would pose any kind of major problem. Oh…did I mention I was assigned to a second-grade classroom?

Within the first few hours of being in that classroom, I knew instinctively that teaching in an elementary school was not in my future. I found the multitasking aspect of the job exhausting at best and unmanageable at worst. There were so many demands I had to deal with at the same time, and I didn't know which way to turn my attention first. By the time I completed the first demand, I had totally forgotten about all the others. My cooperating teacher was always complaining about my poor job performance and she was making it clear my future as a teacher was in jeopardy. A month into student teaching, my dream of being a teacher was shattered. I voluntary quit the student teaching program, even though it is not in my nature to be a quitter.

After that, I essentially had to go back to the drawing board to figure out what I was going to do next. In looking back on my life, it was this horrific experience of student teaching that ultimately led me to seek a diagnosis of Asperger Syndrome, which I obtained the following year in 2004 at the age of 27.

I have great respect for those in the teaching profession. My firsthand experience as a student teacher, if nothing else, taught me that the job of teaching is not an easy one! With that said, I am going to ask teachers to reflect beyond their important role of teaching academics. I believe a teacher's role should not be confined to teaching the core subjects requested of them. The responsibility of being a teacher also extends to creating a classroom atmosphere that is like a family. Students in the United States spend approximately a thousand hours in school every year. With the amount of time students spend together, it is vitally important for everyone in the class to feel included and welcome.

Looking at the child with Asperger Syndrome, it is easy to see where school can seem like a foreign environment. The social difficulties along with the environmental stressors can be depleting for the child with Asperger's to deal with on a daily basis. In addition, the Asperger child spends over a thousand hours a year in a place where he or she is socially excluded, teased, verbally abused, and often physically victimized on a regular basis.

This chapter will examine the role of the teacher as a problem solver. The aim is to help teachers understand how children with Asperger Syndrome think and process the world around them, and it is hoped that this will encourage teachers to build strong alliances between themselves and their Asperger students.

Teacher awareness

Most teachers do not report bullying as one of the more problematic student behaviors they encounter (Glynn and Wheldall 1989; Gray and Sime 1989). The most frequently reported behavior problem they mention is children talking out of turn. Clearly, this indicates that teacher awareness of bullying behavior needs to increase. It is evident throughout the research that the issue of bullying is often unrecognized and minimized by teachers (Olweus 1993). Many teachers fail to see that bullying is a serious problem in their schools even when it clearly exists. Perhaps more disturbing is that children who attempt to bully in front of adults are actually reinforced for their inappropriate behavior when an adult does not intervene (Davis 2005). Many children report that teachers know about the bullying that takes place but choose not to deal with it (Ross 2003). I have heard some teachers say that it's not their job to act as "social referees."

The most common complaint that teachers express today is that they feel pressured about their students' performance on state and/or nation-wide mandated tests. That constant pressure, they say, makes other concerns take a backseat. When state funding depends upon how well teachers prepare students for these tests, it is understandable why many teachers feel worn down by this responsibility.

Most bullying does not take place in the presence of authorities at school. Research tells us that teachers only intervene 14 percent of the time when bullying takes place in school and only 4 percent when bullying happens in the playground (Craig and Pepler 2000). Goldbloom (2001) mentions a study done in Toronto where 120 hours of surveillance video was captured on tape from various schools in the area. In 20 percent of the instances, bystanders reinforced the bullying through verbal abuse, and in 54 percent of the cases, they reinforced the bully by simply not doing anything. In only 25 percent of the incidents did peers intervene on behalf of the victims. Sadly, this study illustrates what can happen when bullying takes place outside of a teacher's line of vision.

When bullying takes place and adults *are* present and within viewing distance of the bullying, it is hard to believe that they sometimes do not intervene. If children are bullied in the presence of adults who *choose* not to take action, this lack of responsibility sends a dangerous message to all the children (Davis 2005). The message is that bullying is an acceptable behavior and has been condoned by authority figures. Children are not stupid. If a bully sees that an adult is "turning a blind eye" then the bully will interpret this lack of interest as a sign of approval. Furthermore, if the bystanders do not actively see the teacher condemn bullying, they will undoubtedly interpret this non-involvement as a sign of approval.

Who are the targets?

In an interesting study (Hoover and Oliver 1996) of fourth through twelfth grade, males in the Midwest were asked to name reasons why certain students were bullied. The top five were:

- didn't fit in
- physical weakness
- short tempered
- who their friends were
- clothing (p.13).

Do these characteristics sound like a particular population? Many students with Asperger Syndrome will fit most of these traits. They are often short tempered and prone to having meltdowns. Davis (2005) echoes the fact that children who are bullied have little social support and are likely to become targets. Children with Asperger's display "cultural illiteracy" in many ways and certainly will not wear the latest designer clothes. In addition, motor difficulties can make people with the syndrome appear physically weak or awkward, especially during gym class or at recess.

Teacher support

Most teachers will admit that they have favorites as well as students that they dislike. What if a teacher dislikes a child with Asperger's? When that happens, it creates an untenable situation for the child. Not only does the child feel ostracized by his or her peers, but the one person who is actually paid to act as a nurturer and protector rejects the child. This scenario can become dangerous if the child lacks protection from peer bystanders, but also his or her teacher, who may be less likely to intervene on the child's behalf due to a conscious or unconscious dislike of the child. Let's look at a story that will illustrate this point.

The teacher, Mrs. McKinney, arrives at school one morning in a tired state. She was up late grading papers the night before and has very little energy. As she walks into the building to grab her usual cup of coffee in the teacher's lounge, Michael, 15, who has Asperger's, is there to greet her at the door. "Did you grade my test last night?"

Mrs. McKinney is clearly irritated by this question but does her best to keep her cool. "Yes, Michael, I did, but I don't recall offhand what your score was. And remember, we talked about this! When I'm not in the classroom, this is my personal time."

Michael cannot believe she doesn't remember his test score. "What do you mean you don't recall? You only have 17 students in the class. You *have* to remember."

Once again, struggling to keep her cool, she replies, "Well, I'm sorry, I don't. Now if you'll excuse me."

But Michael isn't through. "But I wanted to know my grade before lunch so I could call home and tell my dad."

She's had it. "Well, Michael, you're just going to have to wait like everyone else."

Later that day as the class is doing math group work, Michael raises his hand. "Mrs. McKinney, I don't see the point of doing these dumb assignments. I'm never going to use any of this stuff anyway."

Mrs. McKinney doesn't know how to respond calmly to such bluntness. "Michael, you are not the teacher, I am. You do not decide what goes on in this classroom. Now get back to work."

There may have been some underlying reasons for Michael's annoying behavior that Mrs. McKinney is not aware of. Because of his social anxiety, Michael felt nervous about being forced to do group work and was simply trying to get out of it in the only way he knew how. Also, working in a group lowered Michael's frustration tolerance to the point where his comments were somewhat uncontrollable. Michael's honesty and bluntness in talking about the stupid assignments came across as rude. The social consequences for making such a statement are that he might alienate his classmates and would definitely annoy his teacher.

This situation illustrates how Michael's social skills are clearly not at an age-appropriate level. Most 15-year-olds would be able to recognize that teachers need their space at the beginning of the school day. While it wouldn't be out of the ordinary for a student to say hello to a teacher before school started, Michael's conduct bordered on harassment. He not only expected her to know his grade off the top of her head, but then he became angry with her when she didn't. His anxiety blinded him to the fact that he was acting in an offensive manner.

Assuming that his teacher doesn't know about Michael's diagnosis, it is likely that she would have a biased view of him. Mrs. McKinney could rationally dislike Michael, which would impact the way she might treat him in front of the other students. She might act annoyed whenever he opens his mouth, and she could complain about him in the teachers' lounge. She may even unconsciously turn into a passive bully towards him.

The main point is teachers need to maintain a positive relationship with all of their students, especially those with Asperger's who tend to be very sensitive to any negativity that is directed towards them. Here are some types of behaviors that Asperger students may innocently do that could legitimately annoy a teacher:

- tell a teacher that an assignment is stupid
- refuse to do an assignment or participate in an activity unless explicitly told how it is relevant to their lives
- become overwhelmed from a sensory standpoint and try to diffuse this feeling through bizarre physical movements that could then be distracting
- act upset or confused when changes in the schedule occur
- need constant reassurance and guidance that could exhaust a teacher's mental and emotional resources.

Given these challenges, teachers with Asperger students need to be extra patient and:

- explain the purpose of each assignment and why it is necessary
- be understanding of the physical movements Asperger students might make to diffuse their sensory overload; certainly, they should not be publicly condemned or criticized which would only add to the student's embarrassment and perhaps give bullies an idea for further attacks
- when giving criticism to a child with Asperger Syndrome, teachers should make sure it is constructive and logical; otherwise, the teacher should be prepared for an argument.

Endorsing or co-signing bullying

It can be all too easy for teachers to overlook a neurological difference and attribute the cause of the child's behavior to a character defect. Many Asperger Syndrome students (myself included) have been accused of being lazy and not trying hard enough in certain situations where too many demands are being made at once (Gillberg 2002). Problems with executive function and concentration can sometimes create the appearance of laziness, which is often comorbid, or associated with Attention Deficit Hyperactivity Disorder (ADHD).

School is clearly a place where being able to multitask is necessary for a student to be successful. A person may have seven classes in middle or high school on a given day and the ability to transition from one to the other without becoming overwhelmed is crucial. Since this skill of transitioning does not come naturally for the person with Asperger's, it can appear that the child is not making an effort.

Teachers who become antagonistic towards their Asperger students because of this perceived lack of effort may unintentionally inflict quite a bit of harm. Speaking from my own experience, there were many teachers throughout school who told me that I wasn't trying hard enough. In sixth grade, I took a required home economics class where one of our assignments was to make a pillow. I tried my best but since my fine motor skills were significantly impaired, my final work product looked more like shredded tissue than a pillow. The teacher, Mrs. B, harassed me every day, claiming that I wasn't putting forth enough effort. I felt terrible about myself for letting her down and my self-esteem plummeted. In order to prove to Mrs. B that I was trying my best, I took the pillow home to have my grandmother, who was an expert seamstress, finish it. Even though the pillow I turned in looked pretty decent, I still received a grade of a D minus.

Many of my teachers used to harp on about the fact that my handwriting was so messy. They couldn't understand how I could be so verbally fluent and yet have such sloppy handwriting. For many years, I endured verbal abuse from these teachers. If only I had had access to a laptop computer, this problem would have been immediately solved as was proved to be the case when I was in college. I could have avoided years of unnecessary criticism about something I could do nothing about: my poor handwriting.

Sometimes, my frustration towards these teachers would turn to anger for giving me such a hard time. When that happened, it gave them, at least from my perception, even more reason not to like me. So not only was I having a hard time fitting in socially with my classmates, but many of my teachers (especially in middle school) seemed to dislike me as well.

I can remember being bullied in middle school in the presence of various teachers who abdicated their responsibility to intervene on my behalf. Interestingly, the teachers who did intervene were the ones who had established some rapport with me.

The bottom line is that a child with Asperger Syndrome will need a teacher who understands his or her differences and is willing to take the time to make a positive connection with the child. If there is even a hint of negativity towards him or her, the other children will pick up the teacher's frustration with the Asperger child, which could then reasonably lead to instances of bullying.

Returning to the scenario of Mrs. McKinney and Michael, it is likely that Michael's classmates will realize that the teacher doesn't especially care for him. The cardinal sin a teacher can commit is allowing other students to become aware that he or she does not like a particular student. It is one thing for someone not to be liked by some or most classmates, but it's far more hurtful to be publicly disliked by an authority figure, such as a teacher or a principal.

Use a strength-based approach

One way for teachers to avoid power struggles with Asperger students is to create a strength-based curriculum for those students. Many individuals with Asperger's are tired of being told what they cannot do. Individualized Education Plans (IEPs) are usually deficit-driven, which forces the teacher to address the student's weaknesses while ignoring his or her strengths. If the student is weak in math and handwriting, most of the school day will be spent remediating those two subjects. IEPs require very specific goals for demonstrating improvement in areas of weaknesses. For example, a common annual goal for a third grader with handwriting difficulties might be: "Jimmy will write three sentences in a row with all of his letters fitting in between the lines." The more difficulty Jimmy has reaching this goal, the more time he will be expected and forced to spend on it. This is deficit-driven education at its worst.

While I believe IEPs are important in guaranteeing certain rights for people with disabilities, I don't believe they should ever be used against the student. Maybe Jimmy isn't neurologically wired to write three sentences in a row with all his letters fitting in between the lines, but maybe he has the potential to be a good keyboardist at the computer. Should teachers spend time trying to get Jimmy to do something that he may not ever be capable of or should more time be spent in finding proper accommodations to tap into Jimmy's strengths?

Teachers should make sure that a child's IEP goals are reasonable and should make any concerns known at both the annual and the three-year re-evaluation meetings. It is not only important from the standpoint of helping the student achieve success, but it's essential in terms of avoiding future power struggles between parents, teachers, and students. The situation with Jimmy could easily escalate if he perceives his teacher to be "bullying" him into trying to do something he is genuinely incapable of doing. This is exactly how I felt when I was being told that I wasn't trying hard enough to make the pillow or write legibly.

Self-report measures/Modified Peer Nomination Inventory

Self-report measures are anonymous inventories filled out by students that help teachers identify who are the victims and bullies in the classroom. One measure to note is the Modified Peer Nomination Inventory (Perry *et al.* 1988). Each student is given a form with some generalized statements that can be categorized into three groups:

- *Filler items:* Positive statements children make about other classmates, e.g. "He's got a lot of friends," or statements that don't belong in the victimization or aggression categories, e.g. "He's always losing things."
- *Victimization items:* Statements that might indicate why the student is being victimized, e.g. "He gets picked on a lot because he isn't good at sports."
- *Aggression items:* Statements that describe aggressive behavior, e.g. "He's a bully" or "He likes to pick fights."

The person filling out the form is asked to respond to 26 items that are listed on the page in relation to the names of students of the same gender. The directive for the students is to place an X beneath the name of any student who fits the description of the item mentioned, excluding their own names. Scores are calculated by determining percentages for same-gender classmates based on how many items were checked off for each filler, victimization, and aggression item.

Teachers are permitted to modify this form in any way to better gather information from their class. Children may not be comfortable filling out this form in the presence of other students. Therefore, it might be easier for the teacher to ask each child to fill the form out in private. Or the teacher could choose to give the form to students at varying times, so that not everyone is gossiping about it at the same time in the playground.

In addition to the items listed in the inventory, it would be wise for teachers to inquire as to where incidents of bullying are taking place. If most children say they happen on the bus, then the bus driver and someone from the school needs to have a talk with a person who has possible knowledge of the occurrence of bullying. If it is learned that bullying is happening in the playground in a particular area where teachers are not usually present, this newly acquired information will help alert those in authority to provide more supervision in the playground. If incidents are happening in the boys' bathroom, a person in authority could be asked to be on the lookout for inappropriate conduct in that location.

Self-report measures are generally methodologically sound in terms of reliability and validity (Perry *et al.* 1988). They become invaluable when it comes to establishing peer-mentoring programs. Teachers should seek out students who are seen as leaders by their peers to be mentors to students who experience social discomfort. Some of the perceived leaders may also be ones who engage in bullying behavior, which could be an excellent opportunity for the bullies to re-channel their energies in a more positive direction.

Playback Theatre

This is a technique that may be worthwhile for teachers to inquire and learn more about. Playback Theatre is a unique form of psychodrama that was conceived by Jonathan Fox in 1975 (Dauber and Fox 1999). It is a very powerful therapeutic tool that permits individuals to see their own behavior mirrored back to them. It has been used in hospitals, schools, prisons, senior residences, corporations, and even on the streets. Well established all over the world in over 30 countries, individual Playback Theatre companies have their own troupes that go out and perform for the public. It has been extensively used in schools for bullying prevention.

Essentially, audience members tell their stories, which are then recreated on the spot by actors in the theater troupe. If the troupe came to the school specifically for the purpose of raising awareness about bullying, the director of the troupe would ask if anyone would like to share an incident of bullying that they have witnessed or experienced at school. Johnny then raises his hand and talks about an incident where Ted was teasing Tommy in the playground. The director asks Johnny to give more details to try to bring the story to life. After Johnny finishes telling the story, the director informs everyone that Johnny's story is now going to be acted out by the actors in the theater troupe. He asks Johnny to choose people in the troupe to play Ted and Tommy or anyone else who might have been a bystander or had a minor role in the incident. The scene is then acted out and everyone who was present at this incident has the opportunity to watch it unfold. Usually music and other theatrical effects enhance the scene. After the scene concludes, the director asks Johnny if he can think of a better ending to the story. He also asks what could have been changed to make this situation result in a better outcome. Johnny says he wishes more people would have stood up for Tommy. A new scene is then acted out where the bystanders become more active in sticking up for Tommy and ultimately dissuade Ted from picking on him.

What does Playback Theatre accomplish? It allows people to look at themselves from the outside as a "silent observer." It also creates a highly awkward situation for bullies where they are publicly cast in a negative light. The aim is not to humiliate the bullies but to have them understand how they behaved by watching another person act as they did. In addition, it helps bystanders understand what they could have done differently and how the "scene" could have ended better had they taken a more active role.

In my opinion, this form of psychodrama is far more powerful than bringing in a theater troupe to do a general play on bullying. Playback Theatre uses real-life examples that the students find extremely relevant as they address situations that took place at their own school.

The teacher or school administrators should talk with the director of the troupe beforehand to ensure that everyone who is portrayed is done so with respect and dignity. There should be no scenes acted out with portrayals that mock or make fun of any student.

The Method of Shared Concern

In the Method of Shared Concern (Pikas 1989), the teacher privately interviews everyone involved in the bullying incident for five to ten minutes, starting with the primary bully. Those who assist the bully are also interviewed as well as the victim. Everyone involved has a follow-up interview with the teacher and then there is a group meeting with all the children lasting about 30 minutes. The objective is that by the time the children meet in the group, they will have been honest enough in the private interview (without any unnecessary peer pressure) to state freely how they feel when they are in a group setting.

Though Pikas claimed this approach was successful in hundreds of documented cases, except one in Scandinavia, it has been criticized by Besag (1989) who believed its major weakness is in not involving parents in the discussion. This criticism may have some validity. It limits the interviews to people who were directly involved in the incidents and fails to include bystanders who could still learn how their actions might help prevent future incidents.

The No Blame Approach

Similar to the Method of Shared Concern, the No Blame Approach (Maines and Robinson 1992) is for children ages nine and older. The goal is not to blame or punish the bully but to establish a harmonious relationship between the bully and victim. Pikas' theory is that individuals in a group are likely to act as one unit, and by calmly talking with each person on an individual basis, the teacher can arouse feelings of discomfort.

The No Blame Approach uses a similar method with slight differences. The first difference is that the teacher meets with the victim before talking with anyone else. At this time, the teacher tries to elicit the effects the bullying had on the victim. The victim is encouraged to express these feelings by any means necessary, including drawing, storytelling, and writing. Then a meeting is arranged for anyone who was involved in the episode. Bystanders who did not intervene are also asked to participate, which is another difference from the Method of Shared Concern.

What is surprising to me about this approach is that the teacher actually acts on behalf of the victim at the group meeting. The teacher tells the group something to this effect: "Johnny has a problem. This is what's bothering him." After the group meeting, each individual is spoken to in private with the emphasis on coming up with ideas about what can be done to help the victim. Again, the teacher does not blame or condemn but instead tries to offer constructive encouragement and feedback. Maines and Robinson (1992) claim a 100 percent success rate for elementary-school children and a 97 percent success rate for secondary-school students.

What are the pros and cons of these approaches when dealing with children who have Asperger Syndrome? Both approaches seem highly sensitive to the victim's perspective. They allow the victim's voice to be heard in a slightly different way. For the child with Asperger's who has a hard time articulating his or her feelings on the spot, the No Blame Approach avoids this problem. The teacher does the talking for the student, alleviating fears that the Asperger child may have of confronting the bully. It allows everyone's voice to be heard in a safe and caring environment. Furthermore, the group meetings for both approaches are conducted in a non-confrontational manner where no one should feel threatened. The victim and teacher form an alliance through self-disclosure and gentle questioning, which would be important for a child with Asperger's.

While I like the non-confrontational nature of these approaches, I don't think they tackle the root problem. These approaches deal with incidents on a case-by-case basis and are reactive as opposed to proactive. Bullying prevention should be integrated into a school's curriculum and these approaches only deal with bullying occurrences after the fact. Most of the time, incidents will go unreported, which means that the majority of cases go unchecked. By including bullying prevention into the curriculum, it is likely that students will be more conscious of their actions on a day-by-day basis.

I also believe that it can be counterproductive to have a teacher talk for a student, even a student with Asperger's, which the No Blame Approach advocates. The implication is that the student isn't competent enough to speak for himself or herself, which could create more teasing and bullying. Teachers should be involved, but they should work with the victims in helping them to become their own advocates.

Bully courts

A group of secondary-school students were interviewed as to what punishments they believed were most appropriate for bullies. The majority of them said that suspensions were useless and that the punishment should be more visible, such as an apology made to the entire school (Ross 2003). This finding may seem far fetched, but a study was conducted in the United Kingdom where they implemented the use of a bully court system. This study, which was done by Mahdavi and Smith (2002), tracked incidents of bullying over a four-month period while implementing the system of bully courts.

It should be noted that cases are tried among peers who attend the school. Mahdavi and Smith (2002) reported that 20 out of 28 bullies who were tried in bully court stated that they would never display bullying behavior again as a result of having been tried.

Bully boxes

Bully courts are an extreme way to make bullying behavior more visible among a student body. A less extreme approach is a bully box. At lunchtime or during free hours, students can write out a formal petition to speak with a teacher or administrator of their choice to discuss the matter. The student drops the note in the bully box, and the person requested contacts the student who wrote the petition. There are several variations of this idea that I believe should be considered.

First, teachers should encourage bystanders who would not feel comfortable verbally reporting an incident to use the bully boxes. Though not as ideal as a real-time verbal report where action can be taken immediately, this procedure still serves the purpose of getting more bystanders involved. For bystanders who may wish to remain anonymous and would otherwise not come forward if the bully box weren't there, it serves as an ideal alternative to real-time reporting.

Second, many children with Asperger Syndrome often act impulsively when being bullied, or they may have no reaction at all (Gillberg 2002). In other words, students with Asperger's may not know exactly how to react or how to process an incident of bullying. As discussed earlier, they may be confused as to how to differentiate true bullying from playful teasing. Having a bully box allows the teacher to create a concrete plan so that the person with Asperger's can talk to a teacher or administrator when he or she is ready to do so and perhaps get a reality check on what transpired. Teachers should instruct those with Asperger's not to react impulsively and to talk to a teacher about the incident, either in person or through writing. Since asking for help is something that might not come naturally to an individual with Asperger Syndrome (Delfos 2005), these children should receive direct instruction as to the available options after being bullied.

Conflict management

Conflict management tries to instill in students the opportunity for peaceful resolution with minimal adult intervention. When a bullying incident arises, both parties (bully and victim) meet with student conflict managers to talk about what happened. Conflict managers are elected by their peers. Prothrow-Stith (1991) reported that most students who are chosen, according to teachers, are the popular ones, although some may be bullies. I think the decision as to who should become a conflict manager should remain in the discretion of teachers, and should be based on classroom observation and the self-report measures the students filled out.

Managers are supposed to be completely non-judgmental and act as peacemakers as opposed to referees or policemen. The managers are responsible for writing down any solutions that both parties come up with, no matter how unrealistic they may be. Then the managers help both parties consider certain ideas so there can be some sort of a compromise reached.

There are several reasons why I hesitate to recommend this approach as far as Asperger students are concerned. As previously discussed, people with Asperger's tend to be rigid, black-and-white thinkers. They can also be prone to meltdowns when they're under a lot of pressure, particularly of an interpersonal nature. Speaking to students (conflict managers) with whom they do not feel personally comfortable may cause them to experience unnecessary anxiety. Also, it would be unfair to expect someone who isn't trained in Asperger's to understand why a meltdown is taking place or why someone is being extremely rigid. These types of matters, in my judgment, should be left to trained adults who have a good understanding on matters relating to autism and Asperger Syndrome. It is a lot to expect of a 13- or 14-year-old student to handle a conflict between someone with Asperger Syndrome and a neurotypical. The conflict manager has to interpret two essentially different ways of perceiving the world. This is a difficult task to perform without the necessary training of a professional.

Token economies

I recently was invited to be the keynote speaker at a suburban Detroit high school for the "SOS" award ceremony. SOS stands for respect for *self, others,* and *school.*

The SOS program was basically a token economy system that was in place at this high school. The way it worked was that each class at the school (freshman, sophomore, junior, and senior) competed against each other to be the SOS champions. Every time somebody displayed behavior that was courteous and an adult happened to witness it, they scored a point for their class. At the end of the year, the class that racked up the most points was deemed the winner. Their reward was a day off from school.

What surprised and delighted me about this approach was how seriously the students at the school took SOS. They all wanted to win! The junior class, who happened to be the winners, were extremely proud of themselves and took pride in the fact that they had displayed the most respect. One could sense a true feeling of accomplishment among this group.

What I took away from this experience was the knowledge that this kind of token economy could also work at the classroom level. If it worked among high-school students, who tend to be fairly cynical, I believe it would work for the elementary and middle-school population.

Imagine a teacher who sets up her classroom where courteous behavior is rewarded. Students actually display a certain amount of competitiveness about being nice to one another. If this sounds absurd, my visit to this particular high school proved otherwise.

I had a conversation with the school social worker who informed me that the SOS program greatly reduced bullying at this school. Other conversations I've had with teachers at schools where peer-mentoring programs were implemented confirmed that bullying (particularly among the ASD population) became almost non-existent.

The two things that peer mentoring and token economies have in common are that both programs try to get everyone involved. Unlike the No Blame Approach and the Method of Shared Concern, which only deal with bullying when it arises, peer mentoring and token economies encourage and reward positive behavior on a daily basis.

Model students

If teachers recognize and reward good behavior, and encourage bystanders to do the same, then many people with Asperger Syndrome will become model students in this regard. Though it has been suggested that people with Asperger's don't understand the hidden curriculum and often act inappropriately, they do have many virtues that should be recognized. Attwood (1998) suggests that Asperger students can be counted on to act like the "little policeman" of the school because they are honest to a fault. Although students may ridicule this, being honest is essentially a good thing. Children with Asperger's can also be indifferent to peer pressure, according to Dr. Attwood. The ability to think for oneself and march to the beat of one's own drum is an excellent virtue to possess. Also, those with Asperger's generally see the best in people, as exhibited by their trusting and sometimes gullible behavior. All of these qualities need to be praised and reinforced by teachers. My prediction is that if an SOS contest were held in most classrooms, many students with Asperger Syndrome would be contenders for the title!

I have suggested many ideas for teachers and schools to implement. Not all of these concepts will appeal to everyone. My primary hope is for teachers and schools to be stimulated and encouraged to give more thought to new and creative ways for protecting Asperger children from bullying.

Summary points

- Most teachers report students talking in class to be a bigger problem for them than bullying.
- Children who attempt to bully others in front of adults are actually reinforced for this behavior when an adult does not intervene.
- The top five reported characteristics of people who got bullied among boys from fourth to twelfth grade are:
  o didn't fit in
  o physical weakness
  o short tempered
  o who they were friends with
  o clothing.
- Some teachers may dislike children with Asperger's because of the difficulties they can create in the classroom. This bias can hurt the child when he or she is counting on the teacher for support.
- Strength-based approaches help the student and teacher avoid confrontation and allow the child with Asperger's to tap into his or her true potential.
- Self-report measures allow teachers to understand the various roles each student has through anonymous inventories filled out by students.
- Playback Theatre allows students to view their own behavior through a dramatic medium. It has been used successfully in many settings including schools.
- The No Blame Approach and Method of Shared Concern are non-judgmental. They allow everyone's voice to be heard in a caring, empathetic setting, after an incident of bullying arises.
- Bully boxes permit victims or bystanders to report bullying anonymously.

- A strength-based approach when working with students with Asperger's helps to avoid confrontation and is more protective of the student's self-esteem.
- Conflict management can work well, but isn't recommended for Asperger/neurotypical disputes due to the complexities of communication involved by both parties.
- Token economies encourage courteous behavior, enable bystander support, and create an environment of caring and understanding.
- Many people with Asperger's can be held up by teachers as model students when it comes to certain virtues that we all wish to possess.

Chapter 6

Understanding Bullies

I have talked to many people who question whether bullies can truly be rehabilitated. Some people believe that bullies are antisocial to the core and cannot be changed. Others are more hopeful. I fall into the latter category. I don't have any love lost for people who bullied me as a child, but I have had contact with a few of them as an adult. What surprised me was how much they had changed! They were friendly and seemed genuinely interested in my professional and personal life. If only they had acted that way when I was growing up.

These encounters with former bullies confirm my belief that people are generally born good and decent. Very few people are 100 percent malicious or evil. We all have the capacity to develop into our true, more compassionate selves at any point in time with the right help in place. That is not to say that bullying is merely a developmental issue that most children will eventually outgrow. A healthy maturation process requires the right kind of support and interventions for an individual to choose consciously to overcome a predatory behavior towards others.

This chapter will define bullying and identify different types of bullies. The role of the bully will also be explored along with some basic principles of neuroscience, which conclude that our thoughts, feelings, and actions take on an addictive quality. In other words, the more we experience certain emotions, the more we are prone to experience them again and again.

Can someone with Asperger Syndrome be a bully?

Generally speaking, people with Asperger's tend to be victims, but their behavior can sometimes create the appearance of bullying. Heinrichs (2003) discusses the need that bullies have for dominance and control. I would argue that some children with Asperger Syndrome who are perceived as "bullies" are merely trying to assert control over their environment and make it more predictable for their own comfort level. Children who lack basic social skills are more likely to be highly anxious when it comes to socially interacting with others. This anxiety could easily translate into either being introverted or having a compulsive need to always be in control of other people.

In her fabulous book, *Aspergers in Love*, Aston (2003) talks about many neurotypical women married to Asperger men, who said their husbands exhibited a strong need for control. Here's an example of a pre-teen girl with Asperger's who has the same tendency.

At lunch, Sally, a 12-year-old, decides to enter into a game of hopscotch. She wonders if the other girls will let her play and is very nervous about it. Sally usually isn't the kind of girl who takes social risks, but hopscotch is one of her favorite games and she really wants to play with the other girls. The more she thinks about asking if she can play, the more anxious she becomes. Sally does not usually socialize with these girls and she doesn't know what to say to them. Finally, she decides she's going to muster up the courage to approach them. She notices the girls are playing a form of hopscotch with different rules than she is accustomed to following. This observation makes Sally even more anxious. Things are not predictable for Sally unless she at least knows the rules. She says to one of the girls, "Janet, don't you know anything? This isn't how you play hopscotch!"

"This is how we play it, Sally. What do you care, anyway?"

"You guys are stupid! No one plays hopscotch this way. I can't watch this, you morons."

"Then don't! Get lost!"

In this instance, Sally might have been perceived as a bully. Assuming this rude behavior was something Sally did on a consistent basis, she would definitely be viewed that way. But it wasn't Sally's intent to bully the other girls, but rather to get them to play by rules that were predictable for her. When the rules were not what she was used to, Sally had to act spontaneously, which created a great deal of anxiety for her. She then unproductively channeled her anxiety into conduct that appeared to be bullying.

Another reason why someone with Asperger's could be perceived as a bully is that they can appear to lack "theory of mind," which refers to the ability to separate our own internal world from that of others. This is also sometimes called the "me/other differentiation" or "empathetic capacity" (Delfos 2005, p.65). It stems from a basic recognition that other people have separate thoughts and feelings from ours and that our own thoughts and feelings may not always correspond to others. In other words, theory of mind relates to the ability to put oneself in another person's shoes. People who are empathetic have this capacity.

It has been argued in countless journal articles and books that people with Asperger Syndrome have no empathy. I would strongly dispute this statement by saying that many people with the syndrome *appear* to have no empathy. This appearance could be due to difficulties with executive function/central coherence as well as high levels of anxiety. If a person can only focus on one or two details at a time, thereby overlooking the big picture, he or she may appear not to recognize that others have feelings and could end up offending people. Everyone does this to one extent or another, but it happens with a greater degree of frequency for people with Asperger's. If Stan is so focused on buying a birthday present for his girl-friend that he forgets to be courteous to his boss at work that day, it may not be that Stan is intentionally acting aggressively towards his boss. In fact, intellectually, Stan may know that acting nice to one's boss is appropriate and helps with matters of self-interest like job promotions, but as a result of being poor at multitasking, it is hard for Stan to be nice to his boss while he's got the birthday present on his mind. It's almost as if every aspect of his day is compartmentalized and he can't deal with other aspects until he has completed the task of purchasing the gift. Does Stan lack theory of mind? Not necessarily, but it could certainly could create that impression.

Similarly at school, children who have poor multitasking abilities may appear to act insensitively towards classmates and may even be perceived as bullies. Again, in most cases where it looks like bullying, children with Asperger's are either overwhelmed and mentally stuck on some thought pattern which causes them to overlook the big picture, or they are anxious as a result of something unpredictable that has happened. Recall that Heinrichs (2003) mentioned that one of the key characteristics of bullies is that they like to have a sense of control.

When neurotypicals bully, they seek control for the purposes of enjoy-ment and gaining power. When an individual with Asperger's *appears* to bully, it usually isn't for enjoyment or power, but rather for compensatory reasons in coping with anxiety. This point is supported by the fact that people with Asperger's typically do not try to rally bystander support.

In the vignette about Sally playing hopscotch, she didn't *enjoy* calling the other girls stupid or get a sense of power from it. Rather, she was simply terrified that her "social script" would be changed if the rules of the game were altered and this unforeseen event made her angry and belligerent. The theory of mind that Sally missed out on was that other people would not want to be friends with her if she called them names. Again, from an intellectual standpoint, Sally probably knew this fact of life to be true, but it did not appear that way at the time.

I know some individuals with Asperger Syndrome who are the most gentle and sensitive people I have ever met. Most of them understand the concept of theory of mind but they struggle with it, practically speaking, when they experience psychological and emotional stressors.

Children with Asperger Syndrome can also create the appearance of bullying when they are having physical meltdowns. These meltdowns can happen when individuals with the syndrome have had all their resources depleted and the threshold for "losing it" is easier to exceed. I was recently asked by a parent to consult with her son at the university where I am doing my doctoral internship. This seventh grader had recently been diagnosed with Asperger Syndrome. His mother said he was prone to physical meltdowns when pushed too far by bullies. This boy's lack of physical control created the misperception that he was the instigating bully. Unfortunately, a meltdown that is misinterpreted could get a student suspended or even expelled. This is why it is so important for a diagnosis to be obtained as early as possible. Having Asperger's shouldn't excuse this kind of belligerent behavior, but at least it can provide professionals and others with a reasonable explanation as to why it occurred.

According to Coloroso (2003), there are seven types of bullies. For the purposes of this chapter, it is interesting to note that one of her classifications fits with the type of bullying behavior just described by people with Asperger Syndrome. Ms. Coloroso calls it the *hyperactive bully* (Coloroso 2003, p.19). She says this type of bully struggles socially, has few friends, and misreads social cues. He or she reacts aggressively towards even the slightest provocation and is extremely sensitive. Other types of bullies include the following.

- *Confident bully* is a natural born leader who tends to be popular and who likes to exert his or her superiority over others.

- *Social bully* loves to use gossip and rumors to his or her advantage and is socially savvy but not especially trustworthy. Mainly girls fit within this category.
- *Fully armored bully* uses every opportunity to victimize others when no one is looking.
- *Bullied bully* turns his or her feelings of powerlessness into relief by bullying others.
- *Bunch of bullies* consists of a group of nice children, who would never bully someone individually, but find it easier to bully others when they are part of a group.
- *Gang of bullies* get together for the common purpose of the pursuit of power. They don't always know each other, but share in their goal.

The key characteristic for all these types is that their bullying is usually fear-based. Even the bullying that is supposedly for enjoyment's sake is driven by an underlying fear.

The core of bullying

The one element of bullying that separates it from other forms of conflict is an imbalance of power between the bully and the victim. What separates the appearance of bullying by someone with Asperger's from actual bullying is the lack of an imbalance of power. Typically individuals with Asperger's are not socially savvy and do not seek power for its own sake. They look to gain control over a social situation in which they feel anxious and out of control. In doing so, they will often act naively and classmates will recognize their actions as clumsy attempts to control others. Sally's attempt to change the rules of the game by calling the other girls "stupid" might have looked to the other unsuspecting observer like she was bullying the other girls, but remember, Sally is the one who lacked the power in this situation. Clearly, there was an imbalance of power between her and the other girls.

Prerequisites to being a bully

Smith, Sutton, and Swettenham (1999) propose that bullies must have good social cognition and theory of mind skills to engage in antisocial behavior without getting caught. Most bullies try to locate the victim's weakness or Achilles' heel, which also takes a certain amount of social cognition. These skills are also necessary in order to entice bystanders to join the bullying bandwagon. Again, social cognition is not considered to be strong for most people with Asperger's, which further illustrates why incidents of bullying among the Asperger population are often misperceived.

Olweus' definition of bullying

Dan Olweus' (1991) definition of bullying is probably the most agreed upon by teachers and researchers. He says, "A person is being bullied or victimized when he or she is exposed, repeatedly and over time, to negative actions on the part of one or more persons" (Olewus 1991, p.413). This definition again helps us to differentiate between bullying for the sake of acquiring power and bullying as a means of emotional compensation. When Asperger children act in a manner that might be perceived as bullying, it is usually driven by anxiety and an attempt to control a social situation. In other words, these types of outbursts are *situation-specific* rather than true bullying. Situation-specific means that certain events can arise that serve as a stimulus to engage in the bullying type behavior by people with Asperger's. *Non-situation-specific* means that the bullying takes place more as a result of one's aggressive character irrespective of any prevailing specific situation.

Bullying, in its classic sense, is an ongoing, repeated behavior, as Olweus suggests. If John bullies Jason repeatedly, with no rhyme or reason, that's different from John calling Jason stupid because he was nervous about working in an assigned project together. The former is non-situation-specific and the latter is situation-specific.

It is a well-known fact that many bullying incidents are marked by rituals that would clearly be lacking in non-situation-specific forms of bullying. A ritual usually means the victim is forced to do something embarrassing without knowing it. The example in Chapter 2 about the young man who was asked by his classmates to go into the girls' locker room would clearly be classified as a ritual. The irony here is that even though many people with Asperger's are highly ritualistic, it is actually the neurotypicals who are more so when it comes to bullying.

The silent bully

In addition to the definitions of Coloroso (2003) and Olweus (1991), I propose that there is another type of bully that exists—the silent bully. Simply stated, a silent bully has the intention to exclude someone. In a study conducted in the rural Midwest, social ostracism was the second most common form of bullying that females tend to exhibit (Hazler *et al.* 1993b).

Exclusion and ostracism are silent epidemics in our schools and can also be the most painful forms of bullying. Almost everyone at one point in time is a silent bully. If one girl is sitting across from another girl, and the first girl intentionally looks the other way as a non-verbal rejection, that is a silent act of bullying. This type of social behavior often separates the popular children from the unpopular children.

We need to create a mindset for children in our schools where silent bullying is addressed and discouraged. Children need to know that when they choose to ignore someone on purpose for social reasons, they are committing an act of bullying. The social cliques that exist, whether around race, religion or school status, must be viewed from the perception of their power to socially exclude others. Even though it might be more difficult to discipline the silent bully, it still is important to educate children about this type of bullying abuse.

Heightened reactivity

From a neuroscience standpoint, people with Asperger's are extremely reactive due to an enlargement in the amygdala, which along with the hippocampus is the emotional center of the brain and part of the limbic system (Adolphs *et al.* 1995). Limbic dysfunction can account for difficulty in reading faces and judging emotions of other people (Cohen, Klin, and Schultz 1999), which is probably what some people would refer to as a deficit in theory of mind. Heightened reactivity and anxiety are almost certainly a result of the enlarged limbic areas including the hippocampus that, on the positive side, gives those with Asperger's a tremendous long-term memory and recall.

This constant social anxiety can create a fight-or-flight mode and can cause internalized panic that could lead to making insulting statements, as it did with the hypothetical case of Sally. To some extent, this is why people with Asperger Syndrome need to make such a concerted effort to try to slow down and logically think things through before expressing themselves. It is a rational way for them to compensate for this deficit. It is a great adaptive function that can serve them well.

The amygdala

Neuroscience principles impact how the brain affects and mediates bullying behavior. The limbic system is one of the most powerful mechanisms in our brain. Without the cortical regions in our brain, our limbic brain or "reptile brain" would rule our lives. We would be reduced to nothing more than feelings, impressions, and sensations and there would be an absence of higher-order thinking. It's been shown that when the cerebral cortex of certain animals was removed, they were easily provoked into intense emotional reactions (LeDoux 1996). The amygdala, through its own central nucleus, is linked to the brain stem, which controls our autonomic responses, like the heart beating (LeDoux 1996). This part of the brain also helps to maintain our physical defenses against the elements of nature and other external threats. Most importantly, this powerful region of the brain uses pathways that can bypass the neocortex, which is the more evolved part of the cortex. Essentially, this means that emotional responses or instincts can occur before our higher brain functioning has a chance to kick in and take control of the situation. This is exactly what happens during fight-or-flight stimulus. Blood supply to the cortical regions of the brain shuts off and instead blood is rushed to our arms, legs, and other parts of the body. This adaptive function probably aided us in our survival during prehistoric times.

In a sense, this brain activity can present a frightening reality. It means that, at times, we may simply not be in control of our own actions. Our ability to think rationally gets hijacked, and our instinctive impulses take over in governing our actions. I do not want to suggest that feelings or instincts are not important or that they don't serve a legitimate purpose. On the contrary, we wouldn't be human beings without having feelings or instincts. But the implication of LeDoux's research is that it is not uncommon to act without thinking.

Although this point may not surprise anyone, neuroscience can help explain why bullies often act without thinking, while those with Asperger Syndrome generally don't fit into this mold. They are more deliberate and careful in their planning. They recognize intuitively that if they weren't reflective, their amygdalas would take over and cause them to be emotionally and physiologically overreactive. It's interesting to note that meditation is designed to slow down and quiet our minds from both our reptilian/limbic brain and the overly analytical part of brain, the cerebral cortex. The irony is that in quieting the mind, which is supposed to tune out our thinking and feeling states, it actually allows us to think, feel, and act with more clarity.

The concept of bypassing the neocortex needs to be better understood by children who have a propensity to be bullies. It would be a terrific science unit for upper elementary, middle and high school, and it would also help to explain the mechanisms of why we often act impulsively, creating further problems for ourselves and others. The motto for this unit could be: "Control your mind. Don't let it control you."

Bullying is usually planned without concern for consequences. To be able to act in this manner requires higher-order thinking, yet the underlying or unconscious reasons for bullying often have a fear-based emotional underpinning. This underpinning is what teachers need to explore with their students. Students can learn that the act of bullying is behavior that really reflects weakness rather than strength.

If you were to ask a group of adolescents why they choose to bully, probably none of them would name fear as one of the reasons. And yet this is exactly why bullying takes place. Fearing inadequacy, bullies try to make others feel even more inadequate than themselves. Though it may appear that bullies have high self-esteem because they appear powerful, fear is the basic emotional root that triggers predatory behavior toward others.

Receptors

One of the most exciting ideas in neuroscience research in the last 30 or 40 years came from Dr. Candice Pert. Her research helps us to better understand the emotional biology as it applies to the act of bullying. Pert (1997) discovered what is known as the receptor molecule. Receptors are contained within the cells of our body and, in fact, one nerve cell may have as many as 100,000 receptors. These molecular receptors are made up of various chains of amino acids or proteins. The miracle about these receptors is that they are conscious in a sense. They actually begin to vibrate. They vibrate in our cell membranes scanning the environment. Their goal is to find a ligand that matches their chemical state. Ligands consist of neurotransmitters, steroids, and peptides. Endorphins are one type of peptide. Receptors essentially bind themselves to peptides and, once they bind, the cell's interior receives the message that causes it to alter its chemical state. Once this happens within one cell, a chain reaction begins where new peptides are generated that correspond with the previous fusion between receptor and peptide.

These peptides in our body produce many different types of emotions. The more peptides of a certain emotion that bind with various receptors, the more that particular emotion will be experienced. The message of Pert's discovery is that the more we experience an emotion, the more we are bound to experience it repeatedly. Therefore, the more bullies are ruled by fear, the more they will need to engage in bullying as a way to combat their vulnerable feelings. However, if bullies could experience empathy, the impact on body chemistry could significantly affect their future behavior.

It's been proven that altering emotions through changing body chemistry actually works. From 1975, at the Oakwood Forensic Center in Lima, Ohio, certain inmates were permitted to care for small animals, like fish, hamsters, and birds (Moneymaker 1991). As a result of taking care of these pets, the results were astounding. Those inmates drastically changed their behavior. They needed only half as much medication, had very few incidents of violence, and suicide attempts were reduced. One could easily deduce from reading this study that the inmates' body chemistry was altered because of the relationships they developed with these therapeutic pets. If these changes could take place in a prison population, imagine the potential for change that could exist in the behavior patterns of bullies in our schools.

To simplify, the revolutionary idea presented by Pert is that the brain may not be the only thinking and feeling center in our bodies. Perhaps even the cells throughout our bodies influence our mental and emotional state. Indeed, doctors have speculated that the human heart has a capacity to think and feel to a certain extent, independent of the brain (Pearsall 1999). This finding would explain the many documented cases of heart transplant recipients who may begin taking on the characteristics of their donors (Sylvia 1997).

Roots of Empathy

There are several important strategies and solutions that are specifically designed to help children refrain from bullying behavior. One strategy that has received considerable attention in Canada in recent years is Gordon's (2005) Roots of Empathy (www.rootsofempathy.org). Gordon founded this program in 1996 to foster inclusiveness, to increase emotional literacy, and to reduce the levels of bullying and aggression in young people. This program, although designed for the general curriculum, is also targeted to help with bullying prevention. One reason that makes this program so unique is that students become involved in the life of a baby.

A neighborhood parent brings an infant to school. A certified Roots of Empathy instructor identifies the baby's significant developmental milestones and teaches students about the baby's needs and temperament. The instructor covers the neuroscience of a baby's brain development. Students learn about the wiring and neural connections in babies and how the plasticity of their brains allows them to be natural learners.

A 600-page curriculum is divided into nine different sections. There are separate curricula for grades one through three, four through six, and seven through eight. The instructor visits the class the week before and the week after the baby visits. The children celebrate important milestones in the baby's development, learn to care for the baby, and gain empathy through this hands-on nurturing process.

The Roots of Empathy program helps to establish the empathetic peptides early on in life. It helps young children through early adolescence connect to the process of caring for someone who is vulnerable. One of the classic examples that illustrates this principle can be observed the 1988 movie *Rain Man*. At the beginning of the movie, Tom Cruise's character, Charlie Babbitt, is a classic bully. He goes to a mental institution to kidnap his autistic brother, Raymond, so he can get half of the inheritance that was denied to him by his father. When he learns that his brother, played by Dustin Hoffman, has no concept of the value of money, he becomes outraged that Raymond will receive half the inheritance. Charlie kidnaps Raymond and the brothers embark on a cross-country journey of discovery. Charlie clearly can't relate to Raymond in any meaningful way. Most scenes depict Charlie being extremely irritated with Raymond's idiosyncrasies and strange mannerisms. However, at the end of the movie, a breakthrough happens. Charlie discovers that, in fact, he can connect with his brother in a poignant way, and suddenly the most important aspect of his life becomes his relationship with his brother. This is the prototypical example of how a bully and a vulnerable person can come together and form a meaningful relationship.

Peer mentoring

When someone can form a bond with a vulnerable person, it can be a life-changing experience. One of the ways in which this bond can be formed is through peer mentoring. Beane (1999) says that community services for students can offer a number of benefits, including developing leadership skills, becoming helpful and respecting of others, and increasing patience. Peer mentoring can be an excellent opportunity for bullies to form meaningful relationships with people who may be (or at least seem) more vulnerable than they are.

The bully needs a mentor

Normally, when we think of peer mentoring, it is the victim who needs a mentor, but it is also important to provide the bully with a mentor. Garry and Grossman (1997) report that those who were matched with a mentor had positive results in their lives, including:

- They were less likely to start using drugs.
- They were less likely to start drinking.

- They were less likely to skip school.
- They were more likely to get along better with their parents.
- They were more likely to get along better with their peers.

The most powerful kind of mentoring for a bully is to be mentored by an adult who was a former bully. Not only could the mentor help the protégé understand why bullying is wrong, but the mentor could personally share the detrimental consequences he or she suffered as a result of his or her own destructive behavior. This process is similar to when parents ask me to mentor their child with Asperger's. I may get asked because I'm a doctoral student or because they trust me, but another compelling reason I am asked is because I went through struggles similar to their child's and still became a successful adult. My life history gives these parents hope. They see that I made productive choices with my life and have been able to live independently and do well in my professional endeavors, even though it hasn't been an easy process. Similarly, the goal would be for the mentor to demonstrate to the bully, through his or her own life story, that he or she can make different and more productive choices. I encourage all teachers to talk to adults who could be potential mentors for bullies and who would be willing to serve in this capacity.

Descriptive praise

It is important to be on the lookout for improvements in the behavior of a bully who is making an effort to change. When this student performs an act of courtesy and a teacher observes it, the teacher should offer descriptive praise. Descriptive praise is giving a sincere compliment about a specific action or behavior the student exhibits, while non-descriptive praise is often vague, insincere, unearned, and not specific (Davis 2005).

> *Descriptive praise:* Ron, I was so impressed this afternoon when you invited Jim over to your group at recess to play. Good going!

> *Non-descriptive praise:* Ron, you're doing better.

In trying to change brain chemistry and create new neuronal networks for bullies, it is important for them to experience positive emotions when they perform an altruistic act. Continual positive reinforcement is intended to magnify the pleasure the student experiences when performing these acts. This enjoyment is good for body chemistry and for reinforcing good behavior.

Provide opportunities for leadership

Heinrichs (2003) talks about the importance of redirecting a bully's need for power into more constructive and positive avenues. In Freudian terms this would be called sublimation.

Bullies want power because they fear inadequacy, but many could also be good leaders, if given the opportunity. They have charisma, charm, and can impress fellow classmates just by being clever. However, many of them have never been given the chance to exercise their power except in inappropriate ways. If provided with an outlet to channel their predatory energies into leadership activities, it could make a world of difference. The goal would be to create new neural networks for these students, where empathetic peptides suddenly become addictive to the student, just as was the case with prisoners in Lima, Ohio. I encourage teachers to look for ways to provide leadership opportunities for aggressive students who have that potential.

Beane (1999) gives an example of how a bully, who had previously harassed younger students, was chosen to be a guardian for students who had been victimized by other bullies. Another example given by the same writer was having bullies "protect" their victims, so that if someone else tried to bully their victims, the protector would hold them accountable. Beane also recommends that bullies should take part in social service projects where they obtain a new-found feeling of enjoyment when it comes to helping people who are more vulnerable and in need of protection, compassion, and concern.

Don't use golden rule talk

Davis (2005) mentions that using golden rule applications with students can be a risky proposition and can backfire. Asking a student how he or she would feel if someone did something similar to him or her might lead to the answer, "It wouldn't bother me." That response could be an honest answer on the part of the student. Some people are immune (or at least say they are) to all kinds of pain that for other people would be intolerable. We know that children on the spectrum are often hyposensitive: "How would you like it if Billy pinched your ear real hard just like you did to him?" A hyposensitive child might respond that it wouldn't bother him.

A far more effective way of encouraging and establishing empathy is to talk to the bully about the effects his or her behavior had on the victim. Truthfully, it may be unreasonable to expect a bully to say that he or she would feel just as bad if someone committed the same act against the bully, because he or she honestly might not feel that way. But a bully cannot argue with how his or her actions impacted somebody else. Unless a person is incredibly antisocial by nature or does not have much of a conscience, it would be unlikely that he or she couldn't empathize with a person to whom he or she has caused significant pain.

A teacher might say, "You know, Daryl, Marty hasn't come to school for two days because of how you've been treating him the past few weeks. How does this make you feel?" Wording it in this manner makes it more likely the bully is going to step back and self-reflect. Bullies should know the effects that their behavior has on their victims' lives.

Bibliotherapy

The Method of Shared Concern was developed by Anatal Pikas (1989) and supports the use of bibliotherapy, an approach that uses books and stories as a way to have a student relate his or her own life to the story being read. Teachers who complain that bullying prevention takes time out of their lessons could use bibliotherapy to kill two birds with one stone. Lessons relating to bullying prevention could be adapted into the curriculum along with subjects of reading or language arts where children routinely read and discuss stories.

Develop outside interests for bullies

Beane (1999) points out that many students who engage in predatory behavior have few interests outside of picking on others. An excellent strategy would be to find out if certain individuals with Asperger's have any outside interests or hobbies similar to those of the bullies. If so, a teacher might set up a closely supervised situation where the Asperger child is actually helping the bully accomplish a task related to their common interest. The hope is that the bully can learn to appreciate the talents of the student with Asperger's and get to know him or her better. Closely supervising this encounter would be important as the child with Asperger's may be nervous about being paired up with someone who is prone to bullying and to keep the bully's behavior in check. Such an activity could possibly be adapted into a peer-mentoring program if the two work well together.

The media

Parents and teachers need to be particularly aware that today's culture glorifies the traits of bullies like never before. Sadly, we are living in times where violent video games are advertised on Saturday morning television when children, the potential consumers of these games, are watching. The goals of these video games include stealing cars, assaulting women and police, and setting buildings on fire. The average child will see 12,000 simulated murders on television before reaching his or her fourteenth birthday (Dyer 2004). Television reality shows, which are extremely popular with children and teens, depict people trying to manipulate each other so they can "win the game." Is it any wonder that we have a culture of children who are so desensitized to violence and bullying that they truly don't think critically about the subject in a meaningful way? Every time a child gets pleasure from watching a violent act on television, new neuronal networks are created that compel that child to watch more and more violence. Pleasure and violence become associated with each other.

Teachers and parents have a moral duty to explain to children some of the evils in our society that place profit over morality. Beyond that, parents need to restrict access to violent video games and movies, reality television shows where contestants manipulate each other, explicit music with violent lyrics, or anything else that desensitizes children to violence or bullying. We know the media plays a huge role in terms of influencing societal values. We can't control the choices our children will make when they become adults, but we can make wise choices in deciding what we expose them to as children.

Long-term consequences

If we ignore the behavior of bullies and attribute it to "boys will be boys," we aren't doing our children any favors. Research tells us that bullies are six times more likely to be convicted of a crime by the time they reach 24 and five times more likely than their non-bully counterparts to end up with a serious criminal record (Eron 1986). We need to take the problem of bullying very seriously.

Summary points

- Children with Asperger Syndrome can be perceived as exhibiting bullying-type behavior because:
  - their anxiety levels are higher as a result of events not going according to their expectations

- their executive function difficulties make it difficult for them to be aware of the big picture and, as a result, they may say or do something inappropriate
- they have difficulty putting theory of mind into practice
- meltdowns can turn into acts of retaliation when the person with Asperger's has exhausted all of his or her resources and has been pushed too far.

- Children with Asperger's fit the category of hyperactive bullies when they exhibit bullying behavior.
- There are many different kinds of bullies and it's helpful to be familiar with all of them.
- For bullying to occur there must be an imbalance of power.
- Most bullies have good social cognition and a well-developed theory of mind.
- The silent bullies choose not to interact with someone based on their social status. Social exclusion is a form of bullying.
- People with Asperger's generally bully in situation-specific situations whereas neurotypicals bully regardless of the situation.
- People with Asperger's have heightened reactivity due to areas of limbic dysfunction such as an enlarged amygdala, which makes them much more anxious and heightens sensitivity and impulsiveness.
- Many people with Asperger's intuitively compensate for this brain difference by being extremely deliberate and logical in their thinking.
- The limbic area of our brain can actually hamper our ability to use higher-order thinking when fight-or-flight mechanisms kick in. The aim is to advise Asperger children to: stop, think, and then decide.
- Receptors in our cells bind themselves to peptides, which change the shape of the cell. There are peptides for every emotion that exists. The more we experience an emotion, the more we will continue to experience it. The goal is to build new neuronal networks so students actually experience a pleasurable feeling when they are demonstrating or exhibiting empathy.
- In addition to peer mentoring for victims, bullies also need mentors.
- Use descriptive praise when bullies exhibit altruistic behavior.

- Provide bullies with opportunities for leadership.
- Let bullies know the effects that they have on their victims.
- Experiment with bibliotherapy with bullies.
- Be aware of how significantly the media influences the actions of bullies.
- Think about the long-term consequences of not doing anything to help bullies self-reflect and make better choices.

Chapter 7

Empowering Parents

I have often said that if I ever had a child, I wouldn't mind having one with Asperger Syndrome. Though I don't want to minimize the difficulties, I can't help but consider the possible joys of parenting a child with Asperger's. I know that my child would have an unusual set of interests and would probably be very honest and reliable, but I also know that he or she would be a likely target for being bullied.

I have a great deal of empathy and sympathy for parents of children with Asperger Syndrome because of all the difficulties they will encounter. A child with a social disability is relatively defenseless against bullies, leaving parents feeling helpless. Also, when a child has difficulty communicating, it makes it harder for parents to know exactly what is happening with their child. I have spoken with many parents who tell me that their child refuses to talk about his or her social experiences at school so there is no way to know if their child is being bullied or abused. This chapter will include ways to deal with this problem.

The Internet

The most grotesque type of bully—if you can even call it that—is the online sexual predator. With the advent of the Internet, sexual predators have a new and distinct advantage. The process of spotting a victim has been simplified. Predators no longer have to troll around the outskirts of a school waiting for an unsuspecting child to become a victim. Instead, they can make their move from the comfort of their own homes.

One of the most susceptible populations impacted by these disturbed individuals are children on the autism spectrum. I am intentionally warning concerned parents in order to protect vulnerable children from being exploited. Children on the autism spectrum are easy targets for this type of victimization for the following reasons:

1. They are often lonely and have very few friends. If a predator shows an interest in them, they are especially vulnerable to that attention.

2. They are trusting and gullible by nature. Therefore, they may be more likely to believe an adult who is pretending to be a child than a neurotypical who would be able to discern that the person is engaging in an act of manipulation.

3. They are black-and-white-thinkers. They are likely to assume that if a person is an adult, he or she must be good.

Many people who come forward to talk about having been sexually abused report that they were lonely as children. A child who is popular is less likely to chat with a stranger online. Popular children typically spend more of their time with peers. They have less of a need to interact with a stranger or even another child who is a stranger. On the other hand, children who don't have friends are trying to form some sort of an emotional connection, especially if they do not have those connections at school. One of the biggest myths about individuals with autism and Asperger's is that relationships are not important to them. Nothing could be further from the truth.

The lonely child now has a great tool to meet other children on the Internet. It is a virtual domain for making contact with new people. While the Internet has been helpful in bringing many people together in a positive way, it is also the perfect stomping ground for predators who want to seduce the unsuspecting, lonely child.

I am not implying that neurotypicals are immune to sexual predators. Rather, I am emphasizing that individuals on the spectrum are much more likely targets for sexual predators who utilize the Internet, just as they are easier targets for being bullied at school. Comments by the predator might go unchecked by the person with Asperger's, but would probably be noticed by the neurotypical. This hypothetical chat-room dialogue illustrates my point. For the rest of the chapter, I will refer to Johnny, who is 11 years old and has Asperger's.

Predator: Hi there.

Johnny: Hi.

Predator: Whatcha doing right now?

Johnny: Just chilling.

Predator: What's your name?

Johnny: Johnny. What's yours?

Predator: Sam. How old are you?

Johnny: Eleven. How old are you?

Predator: Eleven too. Where do you live?

Johnny: At 3245 Darlington Street in Chesterton Township. Where do you live?

Predator: Do you go to Clayton Elementary School?

Johnny: Yeah, how'd you know?

Predator: So, where do you usually go after school?

Johnny: Over to my friend Ryan's house.

Predator: Cool. Where does he live?

Notice that Johnny answers every question honestly, totally unaware of the *intent* behind these questions. He is oblivious to the fact that it is highly unusual for a stranger to ask so many personal questions at the outset of an encounter. Most 11-year-olds would become suspicious or uncomfortable if someone started to ask so many personal questions at the start of an exchange. However, the person with Asperger's is likely to believe that this person is 11 years old, because that is what he was told. Being hyper-focused, having a lack of imagination, and always being honest can sometimes be a deadly combination, resulting in being gullible, as in this instance. Johnny cannot imagine that someone would lie about his age because he would never lie. He is also hyper-focused on the fact that this predator could be a potential new friend.

Black-and-white thinking

The previous example also illustrates black-and-white thinking. "He says he's 11, so he must be 11." Statements are taken at face value without any critical analysis. This type of black-and-white thinking could also be applicable even if the adult admitted his age. Let's examine another hypothetical Internet scenario.

Predator: Hi there.

Johnny: Hi.

Predator: I'm a friend of your dad's. He told me to say hello.

Johnny: Really. What's your name?

Predator: Your dad and I are really good friends. How would you like a ride home from school tomorrow? Your dad asked me if I would take you.

Johnny: Cool!

Johnny clearly has not read between the lines. He is viewing this exchange from a black-and-white point of view. First, this man says he is a friend of Johnny's father, so he must be. If someone says something, especially an adult, it must be true. Someone who sees the "gray" would be able to understand that not everyone tells the truth all the time. Sometimes, even adults can lie.

Johnny has also failed to pick up on another important clue. Most people, even most 11-year-olds, would be suspicious of a person who did not give his name when asked, but Johnny missed that point. Again, he is so hyper-focused on that person being a friend of his father's that he doesn't sense the person's suspicious behavior. "He's a friend of my dad's, so I can trust him, no matter what." So, what can be done to protect our children from Internet predators?

Get rid of all webcams

A webcam is a visual advertisement for any pedophile. Particularly, it is imperative for children with Asperger Syndrome not to have a webcam. Having this device invites the predator to make contact with your child. A webcam allows the predator to communicate face to face with your child in real time! What could be more dangerous than that?

I am not saying that no child should ever have a webcam. There are children who, with parental supervision, can benefit from this technology. For example, patients in hospitals who are communicating with friends could use a webcam to stay in touch with friends, while they are recovering. But allowing a child to use this kind of technology irresponsibly can have extremely negative consequences, putting it mildly.

Monitor all keystrokes

While privacy rights are important, your child's safety is more important. Buy a software program that allows you to monitor every keystroke made on the computer. This is especially necessary if you find that your child is spending an inordinate amount of time on the computer, and you have no idea what he or she is doing. If your child demonstrates sound judgment and clearly understands the risks of using the Internet, perhaps you could lift this sanction.

Ban chat rooms

Make Internet chat rooms and message boards off limits for your child. A child may protest that this deprivation is unfair and insist, "I'm the only kid not allowed to go into chat rooms." Explain that people who visit chat rooms are not all truthful and that a child who visits a chat room puts himself or herself at risk. If a child violates this rule and goes into a chat room, there must be severe consequences. The consequences must be sufficiently harsh to help children understand the potentially dangerous situation in which they put themselves.

Help your child choose his or her email address

The child with Asperger's should not be deprived of having email access. If a child wants to wish his grandpa a happy birthday, he should be able to do so, but your child's email address must not reveal any personal information. Even something like "tennisplayer1996@aol.com" is too specific. This email address gives away two pieces of important information: your child is a tennis player and was born in 1996. A predator would have personal facts to work with when making contact with this child. Therefore, do not allow your child to be creative in picking an email address. Something that begins with "User" is ideal: for example, "User123467@aol.com." A name that is completely camouflaged is the best possible screen name for a vulnerable child.

Do not let your child have an Internet profile

Many Internet service providers allow users to create a "profile" or a webpage to describe themselves. In a typical profile, your name, age, address, and school are disclosed. Do not allow your child to have a profile or a webpage for all the reasons previously discussed.

An ASD child needs to have an unbreakable rule when it comes to communicating with strangers on the Internet: *don't do it!* If you don't know the person, do not talk to him or her.

Along with the advent of Internet predators, being bullied by peers is another disturbing trend. Being bullied can leave lasting scars on a person's psyche. What can you, as a parent, do to empower yourself? Give sufficient warnings to your child not to talk to, go with, or take anything from a stranger. If the stranger persists, the normal guidelines of running away and reporting the incident would be applicable.

Communicate with the teacher and school

Now, let's talk about what can be done in terms of how a parent can partner with his or her child's teacher to eradicate bullying. Your child may have difficulty communicating how he or she is being abused at school. This leaves you, as a parent, in the dark. All too often, parents have no idea what is happening to their ASD children at school. They are simply not aware of the pain and torture being inflicted on their children on a daily basis.

You must be in constant communication with the teacher. Insist that you and the teacher form a partnership. I recommend that you use a written form and ask the teacher to fill it out every time your child is bullied. This is a good idea because it is unlikely that you and the teacher will get a chance to have lengthy talks on a weekly basis. *You should have this request written into your child's educational plan as something that the teacher agrees to do.* This is as important as getting extended time on a test for your child. The form should indicate where the incidents of bullying took place, who bullied your child, what precipitated the event, and how the teacher responded.

Your child's teacher might not be happy about having to fill out a "bullying report." The typical teacher has countless tasks on a given day, so it is unlikely that he or she is going to be enthusiastic about expending time filling out this report. If only to reduce the amount of required paperwork, perhaps this duty will give a teacher an incentive to try eliminating bullying from taking place.

It is important for a teacher to fill out this form for a number of reasons. First, as I mentioned earlier, research tells us that teachers intervene only 14 percent of the time when incidents of bullying take place in the classroom and 4 percent of the time when they happen in the playground. This data is confusing because teachers report intervening 71 percent of the time (Craig and Pepler 2000). These statistics tell us two things:

- teachers often don't know when and where bullying is taking place
- teachers won't always intervene unless it is mandatory that they do so.

Parents should know the circumstances of every incident of bullying to discern whether school personnel are handling incidents effectively and to be aware of the impact that an incident might have on the child. A given school may resist this type of parental involvement by saying it is not the parents' job to tell teachers how to monitor the behavior of students. Parents must confidently respond that this information is vital to their child's welfare. Parents are not able to observe their children during a school day nor are they able to get adequate information from their children because of their social disabilities. The teacher is the only person who can effectively communicate to parents what is happening to their child. Short of having a hidden video camera in the school, this is the next best alternative.

A parent should not be adversarial or abrasive with a teacher. The last thing a parent wants to do is alienate a teacher. Respect should be shown for the teacher's role and his or her ability to run the classroom. When there is a concern about a child's welfare, the parent should come from a place of caring and concern, rather than being critical and causing a teacher to become defensive.

Teachers must have a good grasp of ASD so they can better understand a parent's concerns. First and foremost, ASD is a social disability. If a child had dyslexia, it would make sense that he or she received accommodations for it. The same is true for any other disability. Children with a social disability should also receive appropriate accommodations. Teachers must understand that an ASD impairment makes it very difficult for a parent to know if a child is being abused at school. Appeal to the teacher's and the school's sense of compassion and responsibility. Parents must recognize how busy the teacher is during the course of a day, but also be firm about how important this information can be in tending to the child's needs. All teachers of a child at risk should fill out these forms, including the gym, art, and music teachers.

The ultimate goal is to teach children to report the bullying themselves. This goal should be addressed somewhere in the child's Individualized Education Plan (Heinrichs 2003) in the short-term objectives and annual goals, as well as the Present Levels of Educational Performance section (PLEP).

Teachers who bully

Most teachers enter the teaching profession because they have a genuine desire to help children grow to their full potential. Unfortunately, there are some teachers who, for whatever reasons, seem to take advantage of their positions of power. Like the teachers who bullied me, as described in Chapter 1, at times they seem to enjoy abusing their power.

If a child reports that a teacher has verbally abused him or her, a parent should immediately contact the teacher and/or the principal. Improper behavior by an authority figure might have been acceptable in previous generations, but it must not be tolerated today. How can you tell if a teacher is bullying your child? Possible signs are if the child is clearly afraid of the teacher or if the child's academic performance significantly drops.

There should be real concern if a teacher calls an ASD child lazy. With everything we know about an Asperger child, the results could be as follows.

- The child will hyper-focus on any negative comments to the point where it becomes a self-fulfilling prophecy (monotropism at work here).

- The child will accept the teacher's criticism without questioning whether or not it is true. "The teacher says I'm lazy, so I must be."

High expectations

Parents should have an expectation that the teacher has a basic under-standing of Asperger Syndrome and related ASD conditions. There may be instances where a child has a meltdown because of a sensory glitch or an unexpected transition and the uninformed teacher may misinterpret this behavior as non-compliance or disrespect of the teacher's authority. If this occurs and the teacher tries to assert his or her authority in these situations, the child may interpret the teacher as being "mean." A teacher who is knowledgeable about ASD can avoid or diffuse these types of situations.

For example, a teacher might tell Johnny, an ASD child, that he's not trying hard enough and he's lazy. Are these comments accurate or is there a neurological reason why Johnny doesn't appear to be trying? Does Johnny *want* to act oppositional or does he have challenges that prevent him from completing the task? It is the parents' job, possibly with the help of profes-sionals, to provide answers to these questions, which will assist the teacher in better understanding the ASD child.

When I was in elementary school and the art teacher was telling me I was lazy, my parents knew this accusation was false. I lacked motivation because I knew that no matter how hard I tried, my artwork was not going to meet my teacher's standards. My fine motor wiring simply doesn't permit me to manipulate objects with any kind of deft touch. Had the art teacher understood my disability, she would have accommodated me in a more graceful and beneficial manner.

A misconception I often hear is that providing a child with an accom-modation means giving a student "special treatment" and not treating him or her like all the other children. This makes no sense. If a student had bad eyesight, would the use of glasses be asking for a special treatment? The same is true for ASD children. Just because they need certain accommodations does not translate into giving them special privileges. The notion of not giving special treatment to the ASD child is an outdated and destructive point of view. The teacher who believes accommodations are unfair should be confronted and re-educated.

What about the teacher who simply doesn't care about students with disabilities? This is a teacher who expects everyone to behave in the same manner and meet the same assigned objectives, irrespective of any neurological limitations. If a teacher has this outdated attitude, it is dangerous to have an ASD child assigned to him or her and a parent should give serious thought to switching the child to a different classroom or a different school with a more competent teacher.

Visit the school

If there is concern that the teacher is not documenting incidents of bullying, there is another resource at a parent's disposal. A good social worker may be able to take copious notes and accurately document incidents, parties involved, and the interventions performed. However, if the child is in elementary school, the social worker usually can't visit on a regular basis. If that is the case, then the parent should visit the child's classroom every so often, particularly if a bullying incident has occurred in the past.

Volunteer to give a bullying presentation

Arm yourself with research from this book and become your child's advocate. Volunteer your time and offer to give a bullying prevention presentation to your child's class or at a school assembly. There are a number of different techniques that could be used to present this information to elementary or middle-school students in an accessible way:

- Use techniques from Playback Theatre discussed in Chapter 5.
- Talk about your own experiences of being bullied as a child and how that has impacted you as an adult.
- Do a scripted role play.
- Introduce the concept of "bystanders." If this concept has been introduced previously at your school, reinforce it with concrete examples.
- Incorporate music and dance into your presentation.

If you are uncomfortable giving presentations or your child doesn't want you to be the presenter, ask the school administrators if they would be open to having a staff training session by an expert in the field.

Staff training

If the staff at your school are interested, they may benefit from a staff training session on bullying prevention. This type of seminar is a good idea because most teachers aren't aware of how to achieve effective bullying prevention. By helping to equip teachers with the tools they need, those percentages could rise. I wish there could be a bullying prevention presentation at every school in the United States. It takes people on the front lines (that's you) to make this happen!

The parent and child team

Parents and children can work together to become empowered. I cannot emphasize enough the importance of communicating with your child's teacher, but ultimately the goal is to have your child relay the important information to you. One reason it may be difficult for a child to explain the extent to which he or she is being bullied is that he or she may be misreading the nature of the teasing. Sometimes teasing is playful, while at other times it can be vicious. The Asperger child may misinterpret a vicious tease as a playful tease and vice versa. In other words, if Terrell says something to Johnny that is intended to hurt his feelings, Johnny may think Terrell is just being playful. On the other hand, if Terrell simply is being playful with Johnny, he might interpret it as a vicious tease and take offense. Again, because of the nature of Asperger Syndrome, these types of cues can often be misinterpreted.

Differentiating between a playful and a vicious tease is a skill that needs to be learned. Children with Asperger's have to be taught explicitly how to differentiate between the two behaviors.

Playing detective

One way to teach the difference between types of teasing is to play detective. Many Asperger children are analytical and logical by nature so this learning technique would tap into a potential strength. If someone says to Johnny, "Look, here comes Johnny. He's the coolest kid in school," the object of playing detective is to help Johnny interpret what the child really meant. Johnny would learn to ask the appropriate questions necessary to arrive at a reasonable conclusion. Questions that most children would intuitively ask themselves might elude Johnny, so he has to be taught how to think critically. The process might go something like this:

- Who said that to you, Johnny?
- Is this someone who has been nice to you in the past?
- After the person said that, did this person walk away or continue talking to you?

Johnny is learning how to rely on past experiences to make a sound judgment.

Since most ASD children are at a disadvantage in terms of reading visual cues, the best way to teach them how to understand other people's intentions is through analyzing their past experience. Because children with Asperger's have excellent long-term memories, this technique would play to their strengths.

Some questions that ASD children should ask themselves when a questionable incident of bullying occurs are:

- Is this person *usually* nice to me?
- Has this person ever said anything nice to me before?
- Did this person continue talking to me or invite me to join in his or her group, or did he or she ignore me shortly thereafter?

The lessons Johnny can take away from this situation are:

- If someone says something "nice" but they've never been nice to me before, the person may be teasing me.
- If someone says something nice and then they act unfriendly immediately thereafter, chances are the person wasn't being sincere.

Role playing

A role play might be an effective technique when one child has called another child an offensive name but it clearly was not intended to be hurtful. The role play could go something like this:

Mom: (pretending to be a friend) Hey Johnny.

Johnny: Hi!

Mom: I can't believe you finished your history assignment. You're such a geek. I haven't even started mine yet. Hey, want to ride bikes after school?

Start off by asking Johnny whether his friend, Tom, meant it when he called him a geek. Would he have asked Johnny to ride bikes if he really felt Johnny was an undesirable person? As a parent, you could suggest some reasons why his friend called him that name.

- Tom was frustrated because he hadn't started his own history assignment.
- Tom was jealous of you and teased you by calling you a geek.
- Tom was trying to be funny.

The goal of this interaction is to teach Johnny that words alone do not carry the full meaning of a given message. Rather, one's *past* intentions and actions are relevant in interpreting the meaning of one's present words and actions. Johnny has to learn how to read intention through past experience.

The child with Asperger's may need to experience some examples of teasing using different sensory channels in order to accurately process the information from the role play. In a role play, the auditory modality means your child is hearing you talk. Simultaneously you are also working with the visual modality in that you're using your face and body to gesture non-verbal meaning. When acting out a role play, it is a good idea to ask your child to give you specific incidents of when and how he or she has been bullied. Perhaps the teacher can provide this information in the form of bullying reports. Remember, the goal is to be as specific and concrete as possible. Abstraction can sometimes be difficult for ASD children, so a good slogan to remember is: *it's neat as long as it's concrete.*

Spontaneous role play

The best way to have this information transition from practice at home to the school is if these role plays are as spontaneous as possible. Life is not a movie where we can hit the pause button and analyze the situation before hitting the play button again. As human beings, we are constantly asked to analyze life in real time. As William Shakespeare once said, "Life is not a dress rehearsal."

First, tell Johnny that a statement will be made and then he'll be asked what he thinks was really meant. Make it into a game. You might say, "You're driving me crazy." Now, tell him that you made that statement immediately after he asked you to take him swimming at a time when you had a headache. After a few seconds, ask him if he thinks that he was literally driving you crazy. You could ask these questions:

- Does he usually drive you crazy?

- Have you made that statement to him before, especially when he asks you for something and you're busy or not feeling well?
- Would you really be driven crazy just because you were asked to do something?

The goal is to have Johnny rely on his past experience. If the answers to the aforementioned questions are all "no," Johnny should deduce that his mother did not actually intend to mean that he was driving her crazy.

Use movies and television shows

In addition to spontaneous role plays, have your child analyze various movies and television shows. Try to choose movies involving characters who are similar to your child. Pause and rewind so that you can select dialogue and ask your child to analyze it. Some guiding questions could be:

- Did he really mean what he said? If not, why not?
- What do you think he really meant?
- Was he being sarcastic? If so, how could you tell?
- Does character A like character B? If so, how could you tell?

Comebacks

Without the acquisition of a basic verbal self-defense repertoire, ASD children are virtually powerless in defending themselves from being verbally abused. Children on the autism spectrum are entitled to learn how to defend themselves verbally. No doubt, this will not be an easy skill to teach. After having been verbally abused, being able to have a verbal comeback might be the toughest challenge the ASD child faces. Impaired auditory processes make it extremely difficult to be able to formulate on-the-spot responses after having been insulted by someone moments earlier. So teaching your child how to use comebacks might be helpful.

This approach keeps things context-specific and concrete. One could easily go online and learn a whole list of comebacks, but for the ASD child, this probably would not be effective. If the comebacks aren't relevant to specific situations, learning and employing them will probably be useless.

Before a plan can be established for dealing with verbal abuse, a child must remember a cardinal rule: *no matter what anyone says to you, keep your cool.* Many parents might be rolling their eyes at the thought of their child being stoic after he or she has just been humiliated. Yet there are individuals on the spectrum who have been able to remain calm under these intense conditions.

Telling your child to ignore teasing is disingenuous. It's not possible. If someone throws a fistful of sand in a person's face, it would be ridiculous to say, "Just ignore it." What a child can learn is how to *appear* stoic. If a child has a meltdown, it's all over. The child will lose the ability to defend himself or herself.

Donna Williams (2003) talks about people on the autistic spectrum often feeling naked and exposed. After being insulted, the "rawness" that Ms. Williams describes probably increases tenfold for the person with Asperger's. Nevertheless, as raw and exposed as a child may feel during and after an insult, he or she must learn to remain in control in order to make a purposeful response.

Even if a child is able to remain stoic, he or she may still not be able to respond to a bully. The child may need the time to come home and decompress. If later on, a parent can go over what the specific insults were, the parent and child can brainstorm appropriate comebacks for the next time that child is victimized. For example, if someone says, "You're a retard, Johnny," you and your child can brainstorm specific comebacks, e.g. "I know you are, but what am I?" or "Whoa…I'm impressed! Did you stay up all night thinking of that one?" Heinrichs (2003) also suggests that every ASD child have a few assertive "scripts" in their repertoire. Ask your child to practice saying these scripts with confidence and boldness: "Back off," "Watch it, pal," and "Don't mess with me."

Ultimately, the goal is to arm a child with enough comebacks to have the bully retreat. If a bully has to work too hard, he or she will usually move on to an easier target. If a child has enough comeback weapons in his or her arsenal, it may make the difference in that child not being a target anymore. It's important to point out that none of these comebacks should be racist, sexist, degrading, or profane.

Of course, if the child seems unwilling or afraid to respond with a comeback that could increase the level of bullying activity advanced against him or her, they would recognize this limitation and deal with the bullying in one of the other recommended ways. The most critical thing your child must understand is that these insults are not truths about him or her and should not be believed.

Summary points

- One of the most susceptible populations to being impacted by pedophiles and their unfathomable actions are children on the autism spectrum.
  - Children on the autism spectrum are often lonely and have very few friends.
  - Children on the autism spectrum are trusting and gullible by nature and are more likely to believe people are whoever they say they are.
  - Children on the autism spectrum engage in black-and-white thinking: "This person is an adult, so he or she must be good."
- Get rid of all webcams.
- Monitor all email.
- Do not let your child go into chat rooms.
- Do not let your child have an Internet profile.
- Choose your child's email address for him or her.
- Make sure that incidents of bullying are documented.
- Do not tolerate bullying by a teacher.
- Volunteer to give a bullying prevention presentation for your child's class or at a school assembly.
- Volunteer to do staff training.
- Learn and play the game "detective" with your child and practice it continuously until your child is able to generalize between your home and the classroom.
- Do a lot of role playing with your child.
- Use movies and television as extra practice.
- Use assertive scripts.
- Teach your child the importance of not having a meltdown when confronted by a bully.
- Execute the plan discussed in the "Comebacks" section.

Chapter 8

Empowering Schools

Growing up, just the mention of the word "school" could make me feel physically ill, especially when faced with the prospect of having to return after a pleasant summer vacation. Life didn't seem fair, having to attend school five days a week and receive constant abuse from my classmates. Sometimes I blamed God. I asked Him why He would make me go to such a horrible place when I could be happy staying in the confines of my home or playing tennis at my local club.

The sad thing is many children feel this way. Recently I gave a speech on bullying at a local library. At the end of the speech, a cute little boy around ten years old with Asperger Syndrome raised his hand. He said, "How am I ever going to get through childhood? I hate school. I hate being bullied. Life seems so unfair to me." My heart went out to him. As an adult with Asperger's who felt exactly the same way when I was his age, I was angry that children still feel that way today. Why can't we as a society evolve to a place where our schools do a better job of protecting the most vulnerable among us? I think it's about time we started to take this challenge seriously!

This chapter will focus on ways schools can be empowered to handle the problem of bullying and eliminate peer abuse. Strategies will be presented for what administrators can do at the school or district-wide level to ensure success in every classroom and in every playground.

Recognize that the problem exists

Every time I meet a teacher, administrator or school counselor, the first question I ask is, "How prevalent is bullying at your school?" Sometimes I hear that it is a serious problem, even though they may have a bullying prevention program in place. Every school administrator needs to address honestly the extent to which bullying is a problem and what is being done to meet the problem head-on.

Successful school-wide interventions

Clearly, interventions at the school level can work. In Kansas (Evans *et al.* 2001), a program was implemented as part of the physical education classes to teach self-regulation and appropriate social behavior. The school saw a significant drop in disciplinary referrals and suspensions, resulting in improved academic performance.

In Italy (Menesini and Modiano 2002) at an elementary school, children were introduced to the following interventions: role playing, sharing personal experiences, and the use of bibliotherapy. Bullying decreased significantly.

A study in New South Wales (Petersen and Rigby 1999) looked at schools using Pikas' Method of Shared Concern. Self-report measures from this study indicated a substantial decrease in bullying.

What all three examples have in common is that the approaches transcended a single classroom. Rather, an entire school system implemented these studies. When everyone in a school district (administrators, teachers, students, and parents) comes to a consensus in terms of policies and procedures surrounding bullying prevention, bullying is likely to decrease dramatically.

Whole-school approach

Imagine living in a county, township, city or jurisdiction where different laws applied to different streets or blocks. This type of system would be absurd. The lack of uniformity would confound citizens as to how to act and stay within the confines of the law.

If you think this lack of uniformity would be confusing for adults, imagine how it would affect children. Essentially, without having a consistent whole-school approach, children are placed in a chaotic environment. What if a group of first-grade students learns a set of classroom procedures from Mrs. Barnes, designed to ensure that bullying does not occur. In second grade, these same students are placed with Mrs. Carney, who has a completely different set of rules. Mrs. Barnes had a rule that forbids a student to touch another child without his or her permission, but this same rule is not in place in Mrs. Carney's class. As a result, students would suffer from a lack of consistency and continuity.

A whole-school approach for bullying prevention is where the rules and regulations are established by the administration, either on a district-wide basis or by each school. This type of approach is essential because the policies are the same across the board and would eliminate any possible ambiguity. Teachers would not assume responsibility for having to create their own classroom rules. They would simply implement the rules established by the administration or district. This type of policy helps to provide structure that children need in order to feel safe and secure.

Based upon the ideas of Olweus (1993), I would recommend schools adopting a Bully-Free Declaration, a contract that all students would have to agree to and abide by. Here's a sample Bully-Free Declaration.

> We, the students, teachers, and parents of ABC Elementary School, declare that all members of the ABC community are valuable citizens. We agree to treat everyone with respect, honor, and dignity. We affirm that no student will ever be teased or bullied with an intention to cause harm. We agree that students who choose to act contrary to this policy should be subjected to consequences for their actions. It is important to stand up for the people who have been bullied and to let the bully know that what he or she is doing is not acceptable. It is in the ABC tradition that we affirm these principles of inclusion and acceptance for every student who is part of the ABC family.

A sample contract could go home to all parents and students on the first day of school.

> Dear parents and legal guardians,
>
> Please read and review the Bully-Free Declaration with your child. Below you will see a contract that we are asking students and parents to sign. Discuss the contract and the importance of bullying prevention with your son or daughter before he or she returns to school with the signed contract tomorrow.
>
> ABC Respect Contract
>
> I_____ agree that I will abide by the principles and policies set forth in the Bully-Free Declaration. If I don't abide by them, I agree to accept the consequences for my actions.
>
> Please print name_____
>
> Student signature_____
>
> Parent signature_____
>
> Date_____

The Bully-Free Declaration should be posted all over the school: in classrooms, hallways, the lunchroom, the gym, the principal's office, and bathrooms. All teachers should be required to make sure that their students understand the declaration and abide by it. In addition, Olweus (1993) recommends that a school assembly be held on the first day of school. At the assembly, the declaration would be introduced to the student body. The principal could assemble a group of older, respected students who could speak of the importance of abiding by the terms of this contract. There are an unlimited number of ways in which administrators can creatively introduce the declaration on the first day of school.

School administrators need to present the declaration on a school-wide level right from the start of the year. Administrators can also use this opportunity to stress the importance of what it means to sign a contract. In the adult world, not abiding by a legally signed contract poses consequences of potential financial liability. Students should learn that when they sign a contract, they have agreed to abide by the terms of the contract. If children legitimately do not want to sign the contract for whatever reason, the school staff should address their concerns individually before the school year gets under way. Parents may have concerns as well, which also need to be addressed by administrators in a non-combative manner at the start of the school year.

If students do not agree to sign the contract, a red flag should be raised on the part of school staff. The contract essentially asks students not to abuse others and to treat classmates with respect. This is not an unreasonable pledge to expect from a student.

Obstacles to a whole-school approach

There are several obstacles to achieving a successful implementation of a whole-school approach for bullying prevention:

- The principal may not be motivated to place bullying prevention as a priority.
- Teachers may not be in agreement as to the degree to which bullying is a problem and how it should be handled. They also may prefer to handle it on their own.
- The rules may not be concrete enough for everyone in the school to understand because of different ages, cognitive abilities, and levels of maturity.

In spite of these obstacles, the evidence shows that a whole-school approach is empirically supported to obtain positive results. Remember that the bedrock of any effective bullying prevention program is that children need consistent rules with consistent consequences.

Systems-based versus principle-based approach

Fay and Funk (1995) describe the differences between a systems approach and a principle-based approach. The former has very specific consequences for certain behavior and the latter examines each case on an individual basis. The Method of Shared Concern and No Blame Approach would both be examples of the principle-based approach.

There are advantages and disadvantages to each method. Heinrichs (2003) believes primarily in using the principle-based approach. A systems-based approach could be a recipe for disaster for Asperger students because they will often break rules without the intention to do so, but rather due to a lack of social understanding. Merely prescribing a punishment for a "crime" could be humiliating for the Asperger student who may have little understanding of what he or she did wrong. What if Jenny, a girl with Asperger Syndrome, hugs Jill and there is a rule at her school that no one touches another person without his or her permission. What happens to Jenny? She ends up getting suspended because of the zero-tolerance policy enforcing this rule. Is this fair? Was Jenny's intention to harm Jill in any way? Was Jenny's Asperger Syndrome, in terms of not understanding personal boundaries, involved in causing the hug? An escape clause should be put into an Asperger student's IEP when it comes to behaviors that might be caused by misunderstandings of rules or meltdowns.

The systems-based approach does help in deterring students from bullying. For example, if a child is tempted to bully a classmate and knows there is no consistent enforcement of any policy at school, he or she may be more inclined to proceed with the bullying. Having a clearly defined set of rules with consistent consequences seems only logical for effective enforcement of the policy.

So which approach is better? I believe a combination of the two. I like the systems-based approach for its consistency and lack of ambiguity, but in many cases, the principle-based approach might be fairer because it tailors enforcement of the rule to the specific facts in question—for example, when the bully is a student with a learning disability, ADHD, autism or Asperger's, or any other condition that would interfere with understanding or complying with the rule or when the incident in question cannot sufficiently be proven.

The argument against the systems-based approach is that it is too punitive and all it does is force the student to serve a detention, receive a suspension or any other traditional consequence that usually doesn't work. Perhaps a zero-tolerance consequence is too harsh. Consequences for bullying, however, can be much more progressive and creative than other forms of punishment for various prohibited acts. For example, students who bully could be asked to:

- tutor someone in a subject in which they are strong and the other person is weak
- partake in community service
- meet with the school social worker to discuss an incident of bullying that took place and what can be learned from the experience
- protect the victim from getting picked on or teased by anyone else for a particular period of time.

Of course, bullying offenses like physical assaults and verbal threats need to be dealt with in a more serious manner.

School-wide meetings

In addition to school assemblies, elected representatives from each class could serve on a bullying prevention committee that would be separate from student counsel. Not only would it be an excellent activity for students to put on their resumes, but it would also allow them to voice their input in tackling this problem. Students, in conjunction with the declaration, could help create a school-wide policy regarding bullying prevention. A policy created by fellow students would probably hold more weight than a policy that came from an administrator.

Implement programs while students are young

Research indicates that children will not fully identify themselves as victims until they are at least eight or nine years old (Kochenderfer and Ladd 1996). School-wide intervention programs may help ensure that younger children will never have to experience feeling like a permanent victim. Children who learn to bully at an early age will likely continue this behavior throughout adolescence and perhaps into adulthood.

Hire supportive faculty

Research clearly demonstrates that established school-wide rules and procedures banning bullying can make the difference between law and order and the terror that exists in many schools today (Besag 1989; Prothrow-Stith 1991). Students who live in constant fear of being bullied have little or no motivation to perform well academically. This point would be especially true for the Asperger population. Furthermore, bullying slowly becomes an acceptable behavior at a school when students see that teachers and staff refuse to take the problem seriously.

In an atmosphere where the adults in charge do not take a strong stand on curbing bullying, children will not receive a clear message about this type of aggressive behavior. Take the real-life example of a principal of a high school in Reno, Nevada. This principal was sought out by a gay teen after a couple of high-school students threw a lasso around his neck, humiliating him, simply for being gay. Instead of the principal cooperating with the authorities to take legal action for this heinous offense, he cautioned the student who had sought him out to quit "acting like a fag" (Kirby 2001). It is incomprehensible that a high-school principal could make such an audaciously prejudiced comment in the context of that situation.

Another example of insensitivity by an educator occurred when I was studying to become a teacher. I took a trip to Oxford, England, for a study-abroad program with a group of special education teachers from the University of Detroit Mercy, who were also pursuing their master's degree. Our group were living in the dorm of a college for three weeks along with a group of engineering students from another university. During the trip, our group became acquainted with the group of engineering students. Two of the people from the engineering group clearly displayed characteristics of Asperger Syndrome, although I'm not aware of any formal diagnosis.

As a group of special education teachers, one would expect some modicum of sensitivity towards these engineering students. However, rather than showing sensitivity, they teased these individuals and mocked them behind their backs. One of these teachers actually said in hearing range of one of the engineering students, "Move over, I don't want to sit next to him." This kind of exclusionary statement is what you might expect from a third grader, not from someone who is educated and has already been hired as a special education teacher.

Being a principal or a special education teacher does not guarantee appropriate behavior towards special needs children. If a school or district is to institute a Bully-Free Declaration and expect students to abide by it, then teachers, principals, and administrators must also conform to the rules. Teachers should be required to demonstrate to administrators in the hiring process that they would not be capable of misusing their authority against a child in any way. During the interview, it might be wise for administrators to explore possible prejudices a prospective teacher might have. Is a person prejudiced against or simply ill informed about certain groups of people with disabilities, minorities, or homosexuals? Perhaps an administrator might even give a hypothetical scenario to a teaching candidate, asking how he or she would handle a situation involving a teacher who abused his or her position of authority against a student. Even if the candidate gives a politically correct response, a savvy administrator can judge sincerity by the amount of time it takes the candidate to answer the hypothetical question. A candidate should answer quickly that he or she would try to get to the bottom of the situation by interviewing all parties involved, and, if necessary, cooperate with the authorities. If the candidate has no idea what to do, it may mean that he or she lacks the kind of common sense necessary to handle these kinds of situations that involve prejudice. The candidate's facial expressions should also be observed. If the candidate seems uncomfortable with this line of questioning, it should raise a red flag as to some unresolved issues.

Discipline for teachers or administrators who bully

Toward the end of the movie *The Breakfast Club*, there is a classic confrontation between the principal and one of the worst troublemakers in the school. In the scene, the principal challenges the student to a fight, daring the student to knock him out. When the student refuses, the principal accuses him of being a coward. That is a clear, if exaggerated, example of an administrator who bullied a bully.

School districts must deal with teachers who bully students as much as they deal with students bullying each other. Being a teacher or administrator does not give one license to misuse one's authority by bullying students. Serious consequences need to be in place at the district level for those who act improperly.

Teacher in-service programs

It is important that teachers are up to date on the latest research and suggested strategies for reducing bullying in their schools. Districts and principals should coordinate mandatory teacher in-services to address this topic on a regular basis. Someone with a disability who was bullied as a child would be a powerful speaker to talk to teachers about the effects of bullying. I have been frequently hired to speak in this capacity to many school districts. A local psychologist who specializes in bullying-related matters would be another good choice of speaker for an in-service. These types of presentations are just as important as those designed to help teachers learn about the Orton-Gillingham method (Ritchey 2006) of reading. If teachers do not have the knowledge and expertise relating to bullying issues, they will be ignorant and powerless in their ability to combat this problem.

Student watch program

Some schools implement student watch programs. Ross (2003) mentions that these programs select various students and have them patrol the lunchroom and playground to ensure that bullying or other antisocial behaviors are not taking place. When incidents of bullying are observed, they are reported to staff. The one caveat about such a program is to make sure that retaliation by the bullies does not occur against these school monitors.

In choosing monitors, teachers and staff should be looking for well-liked students who are role models to their peers. Also, assigning these positions to former bullies under close faculty supervision might help them become more sensitive to the plight of their victims.

Support groups

Katz (1993) recommends that students have support groups at their schools run by staff on a variety of subjects to help further their emotional wellbeing. Research indicates that support groups designed to meet the emotional needs of victims of bullying would be ideal (Arora 1991; Besag 1989). Such a group might particularly benefit the Asperger population who often feel isolated in their chronic victimization. If they could have an opportunity to see that a lot of different people experience bullying, it would help reduce the internalization of blame and self-condemnation they so often experience. The goal would be to share the experiences of being bullied.

Trained counselors

School counselors and social workers should counsel and assist students who are both victims and aggressors in the bullying cycle. It would be important for the counselors to be well versed in Asperger Syndrome since this is a population likely to experience a lot of bullying. Many students with Asperger's will not take the first step and reach out for the help and support of a school counselor. Therefore, it's a good idea for counselors to check in with their Asperger students on a regular basis to see how things are going. Providing support by just being there to listen could make a world of difference for the student.

Assertiveness training

Many people with Asperger Syndrome lack the assertiveness necessary to effectively combat bullying. In addition to the suggestions given in Chapter 7 on empowering parents by teaching Asperger children assertiveness skills, it might be wise to address this need in an IEP. School social workers and psychologists would be ideal persons to help students with Asperger's gain the tools necessary to recognize bullying and to help them learn how to better defend themselves. Staff and parents should collaborate on best practices for teaching assertiveness to children with Asperger's. Many of the assertiveness tips given to parents in the previous chapter would also be applicable for school staff to use.

Here are some more concrete suggestions that staff could give children with Asperger's in becoming more assertive.

- Try to find someone to play with at recess or to sit with at lunch. If you have trouble with this task, ask an adult to help match you up with another student. Generally, it is less likely that someone will pick on you when you are playing with someone else than when you are alone.

- Look the bully in the eye if this is at all possible. Making eye contact lets the other person know that he or she does not intimidate you.

- Respond if someone has verbally abused you by saying something like "Get a life" or simply walk away. Do not talk back if the bully says something in response. This technique lets the bully know you are not taking his or her comments seriously and you are not willing to engage him.

- Rehearse your comebacks or "scripts" in preparation for the next time the bully makes his or her move. People with Asperger's can be successful in this regard due to their strong long-term memories. Make sure that the comebacks don't stoop to the bully's level by insulting his or her religion, family, sexuality, or anything along those lines. Keep them generic.

School-wide Disabilities Awareness Week

The aim of a school-wide Disabilities Awareness Week would be to educate children about individuals who have disabilities. By being exposed to a number of successful guest speakers, including successful adults with disabilities, children can learn about the gifts and life lessons people with disabilities can possess.

Guest speakers

At school-wide assemblies, I recommend the use of more accomplished motivational speakers who can talk about their own painful experiences of having been bullied. Patricia Polacco, the author whom I spoke about in the Introduction, is a perfect example of a well-known, successful adult transfixing her audience when she opened her heart and spoke about her experiences of having been bullied. The speaker doesn't have to be famous. It is important that this person be a good communicator who was often bullied as a child. Ideally, he or she would be funny, honest, and not afraid to be vulnerable in front of a group of children.

Video monitoring

Many schools have endorsed the use of video cameras to patrol for bullying behavior. The aim here is to catch the bullies on monitored, closed-circuit television. Cameras can be strategically placed throughout a school in locations where bullying is most likely to occur. Schools could gather this information by asking the students themselves, through self-report measures, where bullying tends to take place. Similar to what you would see in a convenience store, several monitors could be installed at district headquarters, which would be hooked up to the cameras through a four, five, six, seven or eight way split screen. Alternatively, the monitors could be in the main office of a school where staff could help monitor what was transpiring. The cameras would always be recording so that if an incident of bullying did occur, it would be caught on tape and the bully's conduct would be preserved as evidence of his act.

A civil libertarian might argue that this practice would turn a school into a police state. Nevertheless, I am in favor of this approach if it would help curtail bullying. First, it would diffuse arguments parents might put up about their child not being capable of bullying someone (Ross 2003). If the act is caught on tape, parents can't dispute the facts. Second, this procedure has been tried in schools with positive results. In a Toronto school where bullying was out of control, the school board authorized the installation of closed-circuit television cameras to be placed in various areas in and surrounding the school. This decision met with great success (Fennell 1993). In Solihull, England, cameras were installed that proved to be invaluable in the school's fight against bullying (O'Malley 1993). It must be kept in mind that cameras are utilized to protect children and not to spy on people in denial of their civil rights.

Ultimately, protection of victims from bullies is a human rights issue. If a convenience store can install a camera to prevent losing money because of theft, shouldn't school districts be willing to invest in the same technology if it helps protect the safety of children?

The most important reason for these cameras, with regards to those with disabilities or Asperger Syndrome, is to give these people a "voice." What if Barry bullied Devin in a certain area of the playground while others witnessed the occurrence? Everyone saw it, but Devin didn't have the confidence to be assertive or to tell someone in authority. Also assume that no bystanders came to Devin's defense or reported the incident to a person in authority. If cameras had been utilized, Devin would have had a voice.

Handling cyber bullying

Cyber bullying is one of the cruelest forms of victimization. As a victim of cyber bullying, one has to endure the effects of bullying not only at school but also at home. The safe haven of one's home suddenly becomes dangerous. Individuals with Asperger Syndrome can easily become targets of this kind of bullying because many of them spend a lot of time alone at their computers. Also, they tend to be gullible. They may give away private information to someone without asking critical questions as to why that person would want or be entitled to such personal information.

According to the website www.cyberbullying.org, cyber bullying can involve making vicious jokes about someone in a public forum, such as myspace.com or an online message board, writing threatening emails, posting pictures of someone in a derogatory way, and using a false identity in an instant message or email to obtain private information or to humiliate a person.

Schools must take the problem of cyber bullying seriously. There should be no ambiguity as to whether or not it is tolerated in or outside of school. To prevent cyber bullying, two things would be helpful:

- a designated email address for a school. A sample email address could be something like NoBullying@SeaholmHighSchool.edu.

This address would be available to report any incidents of cyber bullying that could impact the victim's welfare at school

- legal prosecution for emails that are threatening in nature and in violation of criminal statutes.

Suppose that Michelle emails Courtney calling her a retard and saying no one at school likes her. These statements are not grounds for legal action, but they could be forwarded to a person in authority at school who could talk to Michelle about why she sent that email. Taking this example a step further, what if Michelle threatens Courtney in the email, stating that if Courtney comes to school on Monday, she might never see her dog again? This email should be immediately forwarded to the school for possible contact with law enforcement officials.

Any email that serves to bully a person, whether or not it is grounds for legal action, should be scrutinized to determine if there is a basis for punishment at the school level. Just because someone is not in school doesn't give them the right to electronically bully another person through the the Internet, when the threat involves consequences that can occur at school. It is important to remember that if students do not feel safe in the confines of their own home because of cyber bullying, they surely are not going to feel safe at school.

When is bullying a crime?

When should the inappropriate actions of someone be turned over to law enforcement and taken out of the hands of the school? Furniss (2000) says that, according to the Department of Education, all assault offenses that cause bodily harm should be reported to the police. In teenage parlance, the phrase "beat somebody up" is often casually used to indicate that physically assaulting someone is no big deal. Schools should warn all students that if they engage in physical behavior that harms another human being, they will be in violation of criminal law and reported to law enforcement.

Bully files

Every student who engages in bullying should have a file at school, similar to a police file. This is important so schools can keep track in a quantitative fashion as to the frequency with which students engage in verbal and/or physical abuse. It also helps in determining appropriate consequences for repeat offenders. It wouldn't make sense for Patty to receive the same consequences as Gina for the same offense Patty committed ten times, whereas it was Gina's first time.

The media

Media literacy is vital in order for students to make smart choices as to what they watch with respect to television, movies, and video games. Many media literacy groups would welcome the opportunity to visit schools and speak to parents and students about the direct link between the media and bullying/violence. One such group is the New Mexico Media Literacy Project, one of the oldest media literacy organizations in the United States (www.nmmlp.org). I went to a very powerful lecture a few years ago given by a member of this organization and was impressed with his level of knowledge and the amount of research he had conducted. A simple search on the Internet using the keywords "media literacy" would generate many other organizations with guest speakers who would come to schools and speak to students about this subject.

Telephone hotlines

Middle schools and high schools should encourage students who are frequent targets of victimization to seek support through telephone hotlines. Students should be periodically made aware of these organizations as reminders that these community resources are helpful in times of need. Many times, the emotional support students so desperately seek from their parents will be lacking or will not be sought, and those students still need someone to talk to who understands their plight. Ross (2003) recommends both the Girls and Boys Town National Hotline in the United States (1-800-448-3000) and ChildLine (0800 1111) in the United Kingdom.

Summary points

- It is important for educators to recognize that bullying is a problem at their schools in order to bring about change.
- Whole-school approaches to bullying allow everyone in the school to work from a common starting point.
- Studies have shown that whole-school approaches are successful.
- One whole-school approach is a Bully-Free Declaration.
- It is important that parents and children review the Bully-Free Declaration and sign it at the beginning of the year. Their signature indicates that a failure to observe the rules of courtesy will result in consequences.

- Obstacles to the whole-school approach include lack of motivation by the principal and dissent among teachers.

- Principle-based approaches work best when a student with a disability is accused of bullying. These approaches are also helpful when the matter cannot be sufficiently proved one way or another, which is most often the case.

- Systems-based approaches assert that when something can be proved and intent is clearly established, consistent consequences should follow.

- School-wide meetings with a committee devoted to bullying prevention allow students' voices to be heard and help them solve the problem.

- It is important that bullying prevention begin at a very young age so the seeds of kindness and courtesy are planted.

- It is important to hire teachers who will not abuse their authority and who are not prejudiced against any minority, including ethnic groups, one's sexuality, or having a disability.

- Teachers who bully should be severely disciplined.

- Teachers should be trained to handle episodes of bullying.

- Student watch programs help bystanders become involved by assigning a group of students to keep an eye on any activity of a bullying nature and then to report it to staff.

- School counselors should receive sensitivity training in talking with victims and working with people who have disabilities, particularly those with Asperger Syndrome.

- Victims need school-wide assertiveness training.

- A school-wide Disabilities Awareness Week can help bring respect for people with disabilities and foster a climate among students where bullying someone with a disability is unacceptable.

- Guest speakers who were bullied as children are a powerful tool to use for school-wide assemblies.

- Video monitoring catches bullies in the act, gives voice to those who have trouble speaking up, and avoids disputes between parents and staff as to whether or not the incident took place.

- Cyber bullying must not be tolerated.

- Acts of physical violence and verbal threats should be handled by law enforcement.
- Schools should keep files on students who bully so that consequences can be tailored to each student.
- Assemblies should promote media literacy.
- Telephone hotlines can be helpful to those students who have no one to talk to, or no one who understands them.

Chapter 9

An Interview with My Parents

While I was writing this book, it seemed pertinent to ask my parents about some of the issues explored in this book with respect to my own development as a child and even as an adult. The interview that follows is actually a combination of two separate interviews with each of my parents. I asked them the same set of questions and have matched up their responses. My intention in interviewing each parent without the other present was to permit differences of perceptions, memory, or parenting philosophy.

First, I'd like to tell you a little about my parents. Larry and Kitty Dubin are remarkable individuals and have been ideal parents for me. We have a wonderful relationship to this day. My dad started practicing criminal defense law in 1968 and stayed at his law firm for several years. In 1975, he left the practice to teach law and has been a professor at the University of Detroit Mercy School of Law ever since. He took a significant pay cut, but happiness and job satisfaction were more important to him than making money. As it turned out, being a law professor has given him the time to do some very creative things. He has written several legal textbooks, been a legal analyst for different television and radio stations (including CNN), and made television documentaries as an independent producer for public television. One of his programs was even presented before the Florida Supreme Court. Because of all the time my dad and I have spent together, I believe that our relationship would not have been as strong if he had stayed at the law firm.

My mother started out as a psychotherapist, and although she enjoyed it, she realized it wasn't her true calling. She stumbled upon playwriting and found her niche there. She has had numerous plays produced at theaters nationwide and is also a professor of playwriting at Oakland University. It seems like creating an unusual career niche is in my genes.

So here are my parents, Larry and Kitty Dubin, responding to questions I asked them about my experiences of having been bullied.

Nick: Describe how my being bullied as a child affected my demeanor at home.

Dad: You were a highly sensitive child. There were a few bullying incidents in elementary school but they accelerated in middle school. A couple of children called you derogatory names because you were Jewish. We went to school and told the principal we were concerned about this type of abuse. The principal then had a conversation with those who bullied you about your religion and that put an end to those particular incidents.

Over the years, I have learned that you were victimized in many other ways but you rarely told us about these incidents. Rather, you would come home from school and be very angry, but it wasn't very clear what you were upset about. I saw the anger as your need to blow off steam from various school pressures. What I didn't really understand was that you weren't just suffering from the stress of academics, but also from the torment of being victimized by fellow students and even some teachers. I wish I had been more aware of the bullying so that I could have tried to do more to protect and help you deal with it.

Mom: Hearing about you being bullied was always painful. It made you so angry and it made me feel so helpless. Often, you took your frustration out on us which, on the one hand, we understood, but it certainly wasn't good for our mother–son relationship. You could be really abusive to us at times. There were never easy answers. I was always second guessing myself. "Should we call the bully's parents and risk you being further victimized, or should we talk to your teachers and risk being told we were being too overprotective?" I always felt that we were damned if we did and damned if we didn't.

Nick: Describe your perception of my academic life during middle school.

Mom: We were not aware that you had Asperger's until you were 27. When you were younger, we thought you had learning disabilities, which were vague in nature, and possibly ADD (Attention Deficit Disorder).

During middle school, you rarely shared that you were being bullied, so for the most part we were not aware of the daily abuse you were going through. What we *were* aware of was that when you came home from school every day you were extremely angry or extremely sad.

Middle school was an incredibly difficult time for you and, therefore, for all of us. In general, the transition from elementary to middle school is an enormous transition and I had real concerns about how that would be. There were so many changes. You were going from one classroom and one teacher to many different classes and many different teachers. Even though we didn't know then that you had Asperger's, intuitively I felt that all these transitions spelled disaster. As soon as you started middle school, problems around academic issues and the need for more organization began cropping up immediately, but concerns about social issues did not really surface until we received a call from a guidance counselor at school. She told us that you were socially isolating yourself. Whenever you weren't in class, you wandered the periphery of the school and you had told her that you would rather be in elementary than in middle school. That really concerned her and she suggested we place you in a "social group" with a psychologist in the area who ran a group for adolescents with social problems.

To say that you were resistant to this group is a cosmic understatement. You wanted absolutely no part of it. As parents, we felt that a serious problem had been called to our attention and we had to do something about it. We told you that if you went to the group once or twice and didn't like it, you wouldn't have to go back. Upon reflection, this was a major mistake on our part. We were just trying to get you in the door and it completely backfired on us. Every week, you vehemently refused to go to the group and a huge battle would then ensue between us.

For the better part of a year, you went to the group, literally kicking and screaming all the way. We kept asking the psychologist what to do and she said we couldn't let you manipulate us and that attending the group was in your best interest. So, the battles continued until the psychologist said it was time for you to "graduate" from the group. You say the whole group experience did nothing for you, but you've also said, in hindsight, that might be because you were so resistant to it.

Dad: Since you didn't have the Asperger diagnosis in middle school, all we knew was that you had vague learning disabilities and difficulty socializing with other children. You tended to stay by yourself, and I'm sure that made you feel vulnerable to others' perceptions of you.

Middle school was probably the most difficult time for you. Changing classes every 45 minutes created chaos for you throughout the day. Staying organized was also a big problem. Bringing the right books to the right classes was also a challenge. Many days you had to go back to school and bring home books you forgot for homework. I remember one day going to school with you because you forgot to bring home a certain book. When you opened your locker, an avalanche of papers, books, pencils, pens, and who knows what else, all fell out of it. Some of your teachers were very insensitive. Instead of seeing you as a student with learning and organizational problems, we were often told you weren't trying hard enough.

Your life in middle school was on a downward spiral and, at times, it seemed hopeless. In spite of the daily onslaught of academic and social pressures, what amazed me was how resilient you remained. Just when you seemed to hit rock bottom, you would always have the strength to bounce back within a relatively short period of time. I knew in my heart that you had a lot of inner strength in order to withstand the barrage of difficulties that you were facing in middle school every single day.

Nick: Did you ever consider taking me out of middle school and finding an alternative placement for me?

Mom: After that first tortuous year in middle school, we had serious doubts about sending you back and decided to look into other options. There weren't many. We looked at a school that was strictly for learning disabled students and found out your disabilities were not severe enough for an appropriate placement there. Because a couple of professionals had told us you were gifted, we also looked into a school for the gifted and talented where we thought the social issues might not be as bad. This school had a more diverse student population and a kinder, gentler atmosphere than the public school. We were seriously leaning towards a placement there until we spoke to the parents of a boy who was enrolled there and had a similar profile to yours. The mother said socially it was a great school for her son but that in order to keep up academically, he had to be tutored on a daily basis and was constantly struggling with the workload. It was a difficult decision and I couldn't sleep for weeks. Dad and I didn't think you were sufficiently motivated for such a strenuous academic program but we thought the social atmosphere would be much better for you. To help with the decision, we decided to have you tested by the psychologist from the school for the gifted. Her conclusion was to keep you in public school where academic support was guaranteed, which was not the case at the school for the gifted.

Dad: I was always unhappy with your middle-school environment. I knew you were very bright and creative, and yet I observed that school seemed to be numbing you to the learning process. We looked into a placement at a school for children with learning disabilities and were told that it was not the right place and that you should continue to be mainstreamed. We also looked at a school for gifted students and were told that it would be too unstructured for you. So public school seemed like the lesser of the available evils.

If I could live that period over again, I would have looked into a school that is quite a distance from our home, but may have provided a more nurturing environment. Parents face a difficult dilemma when they are dissatisfied with their child's school. If there isn't a better option, as we felt there wasn't, we had to try to work with the teachers at your school in a positive and constructive manner. Some teachers were wonderful and cooperative. Others created many sleepless nights because of their insensitivity or incompetence.

The problems you encountered in middle school seemed to be insurmountable. You got through the experience due to your own inner strength. Had you been lacking in that capacity, I'm sure a move to a different educational environment would have been absolutely necessary.

Nick: *During my adolescence were you worried that I wasn't social enough?*

Mom: An unequivocal yes. I was very worried about your lack of social interaction with peers. Apart from making you join that therapy group, what I did from middle school up until your diagnosis was nag. Of course, I didn't think I was nagging. I thought I was encouraging, suggesting, and doing what was best for you. What did I nag you about? Everything!

I nagged you to join a social group for teens at our temple. I nagged you to call people to play tennis. I nagged you to attend school dances. I nagged you to ask someone to go to the movies. The more I nagged, the angrier you would get at me. Our relationship suffered greatly during this time.

Dad: Absolutely. It was clear that you were always concerned with how others perceived you. I believe that your concern grew out of your experiences of being bullied and was fear-based. Also, I wasn't aware of how Asperger's contributes to social difficulties.

As a child, you didn't like to initiate play, but you usually enjoyed being around other children. So we arranged a lot of your social interactions through play dates. The older you got, the less control we had in being able to do this. Early on, a middle-school counselor told us that you were not interacting well with other children and that we should get you in a social skills group. We forced you to go to this group, run by a psychologist for children with social problems. I'm sure you felt that we were branding you a loser who had to be with other losers once a week. You hated going to this group even though we felt it was in your best interest. I should have respected your strong feelings, but at the time I felt I was doing the right thing.

I did observe that you were at your best socially when you were in the tennis club environment, either taking lessons or competing at tournaments. You became an outstanding tennis player, and I should have understood that building your social skills through your strengths was a better strategy than putting you in circumstances that played to your weaknesses.

Nick: Was it emotionally painful for you to see me socially isolate myself on a daily basis or was it something you accepted about me?

Mom: It was very painful to see you so socially isolated. At that time, I didn't understand that you had a different level of social needs to other people. I kept thinking the problem was psychological and, like the Nike ad says, you just needed to "do it."

Dad: It was very painful. I knew that you loved to laugh and have fun. I knew that you were a wonderful person with a lot to offer. So it hurt to see you socially isolate yourself. I frankly didn't understand why and assumed that it had a psychological basis in origin. After you were diagnosed, I came to understand the neurological basis for the social discomfort and it gave me an entirely different perspective.

I see now that different people have different social needs. Because we didn't understand your social needs as a child, we projected our needs to be social onto you. That lack of understanding caused us great frustration, and I'm sure conveyed to you that we didn't accept you for who you were. As parents, we fell into the trap of wanting you to grow up and meet our standards of success. Having Asperger's can challenge this parental desire but in a positive way. I feel I have learned a lot over the years and am very proud of who you have become as an adult. I take great pride and celebrate your unique personality. You don't have to meet anyone's expectations but your own.

Nick: Were there ever times that you felt teachers were bullying me?

Mom: Unfortunately, yes. In elementary school, your art teacher behaved outrageously. She made fun of your work and physically held it up to the rest of the class so they could look at how bad it was. We had a meeting with this teacher to get her to see that you were trying your best and to ask her to stop making fun of you. Looking back, I can't believe we had to have such a meeting with a supposed professional.

The most painful incident of bullying by a teacher took place when you were in high school. And it came from a special education teacher, no less. One of your special interests had always been announcing. You had always been able to mimic radio and television announcers, and you had a genuine gift when it came to delivering announcements. Every summer we went to a resort in Michigan where they had a public address system to announce the activities of the day. The director of the resort permitted you to make these announcements because of your passion.

In high school, you took radio speech and did well in the class. The next year, there was a follow-up class in broadcasting that you signed up for. Right before fall classes began, you, Dad and I had a meeting with your special education advisor. She said she didn't think that you should take the broadcasting class because there would be too many problems due to your poor fine motor skills. She mentioned that doing the reel-to-reel transfers would be difficult for you and could cause you embarrassment in front of your classmates. We were all devastated. This was the only class you had been looking forward to and you wouldn't be taking it.

In the days following that meeting, I kept calling the special education advisor to see if there was anything that could be done to change the decision. She made no secret about being irritated by my calls and said, "Just let it go, Mrs. Dubin." But somehow I couldn't. This just wasn't right. There was no good reason why you shouldn't be able to take this class! The first ten days of the first semester went by. Every morning, you sat there and had to listen to the announcements over the public address system that you had been looking forward to doing for close to a year.

One day after school you came home and broke down in tears. You told me that you felt like your dream of being in broadcasting had been shattered. When you said that, something in me finally snapped. Maybe it was like the mother who finds her child under a truck and somehow finds the strength to lift the truck a couple of inches to get her child out of danger. In that instant, in spite of the advisor's warnings to just "leave it alone," we decided to go to the head of the special education department to deal with this matter and to right what we knew was wrong.

We scheduled a meeting to present our case to the teacher of the broadcasting class. There were a number of people in attendance: the special education advisor, you, and the head of the special education department. We said, given your long-standing passion for broadcasting and having done well in radio speech, the prerequisite class, wasn't there any way to play to your strengths and accommodate your deficits so that you could take this class? A discussion followed and by the end of the meeting, we had reached a solution. It was amazingly simple. Another student would assist you when you had to do the reel-to-reel transfers. You were then admitted to the class, wound up doing extremely well, and went on to have your own radio show when you attended college.

In terms of advocacy, I have always felt that, as parents, this was our proudest moment. Dad and I refused to accept what I considered the "bullying" tactics of the special education advisor to keep you out of this class. We fought for what we knew was a pivotal educational and psychologically significant decision in your life.

Dad: You had some magnificent teachers. Your third-grade teacher took a real interest in you. She knew that tennis was a special interest of yours and actually set up a tennis date with you and afterward took you to Big Boy for lunch. I can remember how in that school year you came home in a much more positive place. The difference that a competent and caring teacher can make in the life of a special needs student is enormous.

On the other hand, some teachers became part of the problem. There were occasions when I felt compelled to go and talk to the teacher in a polite and non-confrontational manner. I viewed my role as being part of a team with your teachers in helping you grow up in a healthy way. Some teachers were receptive to my involvement and others were not. There were a few instances when I was so frustrated I felt compelled to go over a teacher's head and talk to the principal. I believe that parents must take responsibility to be the primary advocates for their child's best interests.

Nick: What have you learned since my Asperger diagnosis in 2004 and how would it have changed your parenting if you had to do it all over again?

Dad: One change is that I wouldn't be afraid of the label. When you were growing up, none of the labels really fit you and I thought that was a good thing. The lack of a label meant that you could outgrow any problem. A label seemed to be a self-limiting prophecy. What I didn't realize was that a label can help promote self-understanding. Knowing you have Asperger's has helped me understand you a lot better. It has been so helpful to you in clarifying many confusing aspects of your life. Many of the things that I would change from the past can be explained by the fact that I didn't understand what was causing some of your behavior. Hindsight and the diagnosis have given me knowledge and insight that I lacked when you were growing up.

I am glad that even in the absence of your diagnosis, I always saw the importance of supporting your special interests. That support, although good advice for any parent, becomes essential for a child with Asperger's.

You have become a most interesting adult and I could not be more proud of you. So as a parent, I feel comfortable with the Asperger diagnosis, and I believe you will be able to help many people better understand how to help children with Asperger's to grow up as healthy and independent adults.

Mom: What I wish I could go back and change is all the pressure I put on you to socialize more while you were growing up. It made you feel that I didn't love you for who you were and created terrible conflicts between us. The diagnosis gave me an understanding, which I previously lacked, and has finally enabled the love that we feel for each other to be uncluttered by my placing unreasonable expectations on you.

Appendix I

Frequently Asked Questions

Here are some of the questions I am frequently asked when I speak at conferences.

1. What is the best way for a teacher to help someone with Asperger Syndrome who has been bullied?

If a student with Asperger's has been bullied, I suggest allowing that student to "cool down" in a safe place that will help prevent a public meltdown. The biggest mistake teachers can make is to blame the victim. Teachers who do that end up being perceived as modeling bullying behavior or condoning it.

2. Did you ever act as a bully growing up?

I never knowingly bullied another person as a child. My heart has always had a tender spot for people who I see being treated unfairly. Many people with Asperger's cannot stand to witness injustice and inequality. This seems to be a pervasive characteristic of the syndrome.

On one occasion I did fall into the trap of being a "silent bully." Silent bullies are the ones who purposefully exclude others simply because they are not popular. During a week at tennis overnight camp when I was about 11 years old, there was an unpopular boy who was trying to reach out to me, and I rejected him by ignoring his attempts. Since I was one of the better tennis players at the camp, I was not bullied and was highly respected. This other boy was not a very good player, and his fellow campers did not respect him. To this day, I regret my behavior. It is very possible I could have become friends with him had I not been so concerned with whether I would have lost respect from my fellow campers.

3. Do you think that having Asperger's contributed to you being a target for bullying?

It's not that I think it contributed. I know that it contributed. There were so many subtle differences about me that were Asperger related. For example, in my early teens my favorite singer was Frank Sinatra. I used to walk down the halls of middle school singing, "New York, New York." I'm sure my classmates, who were into hard or punk rock, thought that I was seriously weird. I also had an unusual gait and certain people called me the "waddler." We know that unusual gait can often be an Asperger trait (Attwood 1998). I used to tell the bullies that if they kept teasing me, I would tell my therapist and they would get in trouble, which of course showed a gross lack of social judgment. I was extremely gullible and would believe anything I was told. My personality was somewhat eccentric. I had meltdowns in places at school, like a classroom or hallway. I never attended parties because the social and sensory stimulation was too much for me. One of the reasons life was so confusing for me before college was I had not yet been diagnosed. In fact, during the 1980s when I was growing up, Asperger Syndrome did not even exist as a diagnostic category in the United States. I had many other labels along the way, including learning disabled, dysgraphia, ADHD, and depression, but none of them seemed to include the whole picture.

This is why I believe that it is beneficial for parents to be candid and positive with their children about the diagnosis. Episodes of bullying would have made a lot more sense to me had Asperger Syndrome been put into context. I was not able to understand the source of my differences, so I internalized the bullying as something being wrong with me. I wanted to be like everyone else and thought my deficits were psychological in nature rather than neurological. I kept thinking that it was my fault and I just needed to try harder.

Again, the emphasis for children should be on the fact that many people who appear to be different are likely to be targeted, but those who are different can also be some of the world's most creative and successful people.

4. How old do you think a child should be before he or she is told about having Asperger's?

This question is relevant to bullying because it directly affects the ways in which a child will internalize his or her response to being singled out as a constant target. Unfortunately, there is no real consensus to this question. Many children with Asperger's will get to an age where they will wonder why they are so different and may even ask parents directly, "Why am I so different from everyone else?" Giving a child a generic, blanket answer like "Because you're a special person" does not provide the real answer that a child is seeking. Children with Asperger's are not stupid. They know that something is different about them.

I can't say the exact age a child should be made aware of having Asperger's. However, I do know that it isn't fair to shame or make a child's differences a taboo subject. When a child is asking a parent why he or she is so different from other children, the time has come for disclosure.

5. What about the child who clearly doesn't want to know that he or she has Asperger's? In this case, should we tell?

I have met a few children like this, who hate the words Asperger Syndrome and wish they were never mentioned. I've met others who totally embrace Asperger's from an early age because their parents have stressed the positive aspects of it. Personally, I think it is beneficial for children to know that they are wired neurologically different from their peers. If the child interprets this negatively, the hope would be that as he or she grows older and matures, an appreciation of Asperger's would eventually unfold. At least the grown child could never say to the parents as an adult, "Why didn't you ever tell me?"

6. What can we do to help our child fit in more?

Find groups that revolve around special interests. If the child is into caterpillars, find an after-school activity revolving around insects. If he or she likes computers, look for an after-school computer club. Children with Asperger's are not likely to be motivated to socialize in unstructured social settings where they are not interested in what is taking place. The structured setting of a special interest provides a sense of predictability, consistency, and competency. A few examples of structured settings are a student council meeting, a book club, or a tennis lesson.

Unstructured social settings, such as having dinner with friends, sleeping over at someone's house, meeting friends at the mall, or going to a party may not provide enough focus for an Asperger child.

My perception is that parents often become frustrated when their Asperger children spend a lot of time alone and don't take the initiative to place themselves in unstructured social settings. Those parents need to consider the fact that their child may never thrive in unstructured settings. Parents should do everything in their power to scope out structured activities that revolve around their child's interests.

As a child, my parents made sure that my social needs were fulfilled through activities revolving around my special interests. They always encouraged me to participate in activities that were of interest to me. I was part of a video club in middle school. I broadcast the public announcements in high school. I took tennis lessons with other children, and played on my high-school tennis team and in competitive tennis tournaments. My parents recognized, as did I, that tennis enabled me to be a lot more social than I otherwise would have been. As a result of being on the tennis team in high school and playing number one singles for all four years on my varsity tennis team, I was respected by my peers. People still occasionally played jokes on me and teased me, but it was far less than it had been in middle school. The incidence of bullying from middle school to high school went down significantly.

Was I the most popular person in high school? Far from it! Did I go to homecoming, prom or attend parties on Friday or Saturday nights? No, I didn't. But I had no real desire to do these things. The social experience I was getting from my structured activities was sufficient to meet my needs.

The fact that my social activities were limited to only those that were structured caused my parents unnecessary worry about me. They thought I wasn't getting the kind of social exposure I needed to adapt to the real world. Since my parents weren't aware of my diagnosis at that time, they didn't realize that my activities did meet my needs for socialization. The message here is that it is possible for children with Asperger Syndrome to thrive in socially structured settings.

7. I'm confused as to whether my child should be placed in a mainstream or more restrictive setting. Where will he or she get bullied less?

The answer depends on a number of factors. First, some general education teachers are willing to go above and beyond the call of duty to foster inclusiveness, acceptance, and caring. In those classrooms, bullying is less likely to occur. The other thing to keep in mind is that not all restrictive settings are as nurturing as one would hope. In those kinds of settings, bullying may occur during less academic times, like gym, recess or at lunch, due to lack of teacher involvement. Generally, in a restrictive setting, children have less opportunity to be bullied.

I believe in inclusion when appropriate and possible, as long as schools are meeting the educational needs of a child through differentiated instruction and supportive accommodations. If a general education teacher doesn't foster an environment that discourages bullying and promotes acceptance, I would rather have a child in a more restrictive setting. The best scenario would be for a child to be in a classroom, preferably with an aide, in the early years, where diversity, tolerance, and acceptance are embraced and promoted. General education teachers who don't want to make this a priority shouldn't be charged with supervising a vulnerable population.

Every year when I was in elementary school, my parents used to talk to the principal before the year began about which teachers would be the most sensitive to my needs. They were able to take advantage of this service because I was certified as learning disabled at the time. Consequently, I always ended up with the more sensitive and caring teachers. Whenever possible, parents should try to match up their children with the teachers who are going to be the most accommodating and who make bullying prevention one of their highest priorities.

8. Did being bullied ever cause you to think about committing suicide?

Yes. I can remember particularly in middle school feeling that being dead would be less painful than having to attend school five days a week for almost 200 days a year. Fortunately, I never chose to act on those feelings, but they were often somewhere in the background of my thoughts.

9. Did you have any friends growing up?

Yes I did, but they were mostly tennis friends. They were people my age in high school who I would get together with occasionally to play tennis. That socialization was enough to satisfy me.

Some of my friends growing up were children of my parents' friends. For example, my Dad's best friend lives in Los Angeles and his two sons were my good friends growing up. I would go out to Los Angeles at least once a year and they would come to Detroit once a year. One of them even made a very special toast at my Bar Mitzvah.

Another friend was the son of a Hollywood screenwriter, who was a friend of my parents. This boy was also a tennis player, so we used to play frequently at the local courts. My parents would also arrange play dates for me when I was a child, rather than wait for me to do the initiating.

What all of these friendships had in common was that they were connected to structured activities. When I got together with my tennis friends, there was always a clear objective, which was usually playing a two out of three set match. When I used to visit my friends in California, our parents would usually structure our activities by going to see a live television program or attending a baseball game.

10. I've seen you speak at a conference, and you don't seem like you have Asperger's.

I'm going to relate this statement to bullying in a moment, but I have to say that people tell me this all the time. What they don't realize is that when I am giving a presentation, I am in total control of the room. I control the PowerPoint; I control the lights; I control the script; I control whether people are allowed to ask me questions during or after my presentation. In other words, because I am allowed to exercise considerable control and script my speech in advance, I can create the appearance of being neurotypical. Also, I majored in communications at college, which certainly helped. However, if I were in a bar trying to socialize with a group of people while loud music was being played, I guarantee I would be extremely uncomfortable in such an unstructured setting.

What I do when I speak at conferences is very similar to an actor on stage in that I script and rehearse what I will be saying, except the difference is that I'm playing the part of myself. In fact, I recommend to parents that children with Asperger's take acting lessons, and Davies (2004) supports this idea as well. She believes that learning the craft of acting can actually help an Asperger child improve his or her social skills. Davies (2004) also states that she has met and worked with many gifted actors with Asperger Syndrome.

It is well known that people with Asperger Syndrome have exceptional long-term memories that would aid them in memorizing the lines in a script (Attwood 1998). Acting also helps teach theory of mind by forcing one to identify with his or her character as well as by teaching how to relate to the other characters.

Perhaps there is another benefit in acquiring acting skills. Acting, or role playing, can help promote more assertive behavior. It would be highly therapeutic to learn assertiveness by playing an assertive character. Even in therapy with a psychologist or a social worker, hypothetical scenarios could be created where an Asperger child could learn to act in an assertive manner when threatened or when a bully tries to take his or her lunch money.

By learning to act assertively in practice, the hope is that it will transfer to real-life situations. The fact that I act as a polished speaker does not make me a socially polished person. It does mean that I've worked hard to be as prepared as possible for the presentation of my speech. I believe the same can be true for children with Asperger syndrome where some practice through role playing could make a big difference.

11. Do you ever get bullied as an adult?

I typically do not put myself in situations anymore where being victimized would be even a remote possibility. When I worked several tennis jobs as a young adult in my twenties, there were plenty of instances where my employers would bully me and act cruelly. I am careful in my social interactions because of my past experiences.

Workplace bullying does exist, and I have met some adults with Asperger's who have told me about how they are frequently bullied on the job. It is a real phenomenon that adults with Asperger's should pay particularly careful attention to when entering the workplace.

12. My child talks non-stop about his special interests. I think it is interfering with his ability to make friends and is one of the reasons he is bullied so much. What should I do? Should I let him talk about it all he wants or should I try to set limits?

One of the unique qualities about an Asperger child is his or her intense special interests and fascinations. One of the negative manifestations of this trait is the tendency for long, one-sided monologues delivered to others who do not share a similar interest. As Attwood (1998) points out, these monologues are designed to help the person with Asperger's feel socially competent by having something to talk about in an effort to keep control of the conversation.

Unfortunately, most successful social situations require spontaneity or children will become easily bored or frustrated.

The danger of teaching a child to hide his or her special interests is that the child may perceive this advice as a negative reaction to the special interests. A parent who tells his or her child to stop talking about something at an inopportune time will inadvertently communicate disapproval of the special interest to the child. A far more sensitive approach would be to say something like, "Marcus, that sounds fascinating and I'd love to hear all about that. Why don't we finish what we're doing and then we can spend 20 minutes together talking about it." It isn't necessary for a parent to tell his or her child *never* to talk about his or her interests with other children. Essentially, asking your child to do that is asking him or her to hide a big part of himself or herself and ultimately teaches the child to be ashamed of having these interests. The child needs to improve upon his or her sense of timing.

Marcus, who is 12 years old and has Asperger's, has a special interest in dinosaurs. Here is how his parents or teacher might instruct him.

> "Marcus, your knowledge about dinosaurs is tremendous. I'm so impressed with how much you know and I'm very proud of you. I know you want everyone in the class to understand how much you know about dinosaurs, but there are some times when you talk about dinosaurs so much that it could irritate other children. So Marcus, I'm going to give you two rules to remember, okay?"

> "Okay."

> "The first rule is that it is good not to talk about something a lot unless another person asks you about it. For example, don't just walk up to a classmate and start talking about dinosaurs because he may not want to listen to you. Do you know why?"

> "Because he didn't ask me?"

> "You're so smart, kiddo! Rule number two is that any time you want, you can show off your knowledge of dinosaurs through a school project or an assignment. Take advantage of those opportunities. In that kind of setting, other students would probably be fascinated by your love for and knowledge of dinosaurs."

> "Okay."

These two rules are concrete and easy to remember. They encourage the development and fascination of a special interest while simultaneously teaching appropriate social boundaries. If students *always* talk about their special interests, it does invite bullying and teasing.

13. Would you recommend corporal punishment for my child with Asperger's?

Parents have asked me this question at conferences after I have finished talking. If someone has read this book and has any doubt as to what my answer would be, he or she needs to reread the book. Clearly, I would never advocate the use of corporal punishment. From the point of view of a child with Asperger's, corporal punishment would most likely be a gross invasion of his or her personal space.

Many children with Asperger's, who tend to be black-and-white thinkers, may not be able to reconcile how a loving parent could ever lay a hand on them and still be loving. Regardless of whether or not the act of corporal punishment is done out of love, Asperger children may not be able to recognize this fact and, therefore, the punishment won't have the desired impact on the child.

14. My child with Asperger's recently told me he is gay. I'm afraid he will be the recipient of even more discrimination. What should I do?

The answer to this question, first and foremost, is to love your child unconditionally. Being gay is not a choice (Hamer 1994), just as Asperger's is not a choice. Research shows that gays and heterosexuals have slightly different genetics. Many gays experience pain and ostracism from the social misconception that being gay is an affirmative choice.

Being gay and having Asperger's can feel like a double curse for all parties involved. If things weren't bad enough having a social disability, one now has to come to terms with having a sexuality that many believe is degenerate and/or sinful. A person who is different in two very significant ways will most likely experience frequent bullying. The important thing to remember is that there is absolutely nothing wrong with having Asperger's or being gay. Parents of gay and/or Asperger teens should encourage schools to become proactive in promoting respect both for people with disabilities and those with an alternative sexuality. If this is not happening at the school your child attends, find another school.

15. Do you think the effects of my child being bullied will be permanent and impossible to erase?

The good news is that many people with Asperger's were bullied regularly as children and have turned out to be healthy adults. All you have to do is go to a bookstore and look for the various writings of people with Asperger's and autism. Many of those authors are married, have children, run schools or agencies, and live very productive lives. Stephen Shore received his doctorate in education and speaks internationally about developmental issues of people on the autism spectrum. Jerry Newport is married and is an excellent speaker and writer in the field of ASD. Donna Williams, William Stillman, Temple Grandin, Luke Jackson, Kenneth Hall, Valerie Paradiz, Wendy Lawson,

Michael John Carley, Liane Holliday Willey, and Jim Sinclair have all contributed to the field of autism/Asperger's. The fact that most people with Asperger's have been bullied as children does not condemn them to a life of misery. One of the main messages of this book has been to highlight the potential of people with Asperger's so that they can overcome the pain and suffering that being bullied has caused them for so many years.

16. Are there any other books on bullying that you would recommend by other Asperger authors?

Luke Jackson (2002) writes about bullying in his outstandingly clever book entitled *Freaks, Geeks and Asperger Syndrome*, also published by Jessica Kingsley Publishers. Luke is a gifted adolescent with Asperger's who has a knack for relating to an adolescent audience through his writing. Reviews of his book have been extremely positive and I wholeheartedly recommend it.

17. Do you recommend that my child learn to play a sport?

Sports are important in our society. If a child can develop a legitimate interest in a sport, it can help in terms of reducing bullying. Children who excel in athletics fit in with some sports-specific groups. However, not every child with Asperger's will have enough athletic aptitude and competitiveness to excel in a sport, but others may have that potential. My cousin, who has Asperger Syndrome and isn't very athletic, consistently scores over 200 in a game of bowling, which is a very good score. So if there is athletic aptitude and desire, the sky's the limit!

Typically children with Asperger's will excel in individual sports (Dubin 2004). Sports that have a team component often force an ASD individual to read non-verbal cues from teammates and then communicate with them in a sort of rapid-fire way. Individual sports allow for the person to stay truly focused on the task at hand, without the distraction of teammates. Dr. John Milanovich stated in *Diagnosis Asperger's: Nick Dubin's Journey of Self-Discovery* (Dubin 2004), that people with Asperger Syndrome have the potential to excel at sports that involve a lot of motor-based repetition. That reasoning, I believe, explains why I was able to successfully compete in tennis during high school and college.

Internet Resources

www.stopbullyingnow.com

Website of author Stan Davis, who wrote *Schools Where Everyone Belongs* (2005). Davis offers a resource for preteens and teenagers that gives valuable information on reasons why children bully, what to do when someone else is bullied, and information for bullies themselves. Included on Mr. Davis' website are resources for both parents and educators.

www.dontlaugh.org

Operation Respect is a non-profit organization working to transform schools, camps, and organizations focused on children and youth into more compassionate, safe, and respectful environments. Founded by Peter Yarrow of the folk group Peter, Paul, and Mary, the organization disseminates educational resources that are designed to establish a climate that reduces the emotional and physical cruelty some children inflict upon each other by behaviors such as ridicule, bullying, and violence.

www.aspergerinformation.org

Website of author Rebekah Heinrichs, who writes extensively about Asperger Syndrome and bullying.

www.bullying.co.uk

One of the United Kingdom's best websites offering helpful resources and information on bullying prevention.

www.education.unisa.edu.au/bullying

Website of internationally acclaimed author Ken Rigby, one of the foremost experts on bullying in the world.

www.modelprograms.samhsa.gov/pdfs/FactSheets/Olwe us%20Bully.pdf

Information about the world-famous Olweus bullying prevention program, which claims a 30 to 70 percent success rate.

www.tonyattwood.com.au

Website of the always helpful and world-renowned author on Asperger Syndrome, Dr. Tony Attwood. Dr. Attwood wrote *Asperger Syndrome: A Guide for Parents and Professionals*, published by Jessica Kingsley Publishers (1998).

www.udel.edu/bkirby/asperger/education.html

Great website with myriad links to helpful websites regarding bullying and Asperger's, homeschooling, educational videos, sample IEPs, learning disability information, and tips for teachers.

www.kidsareworthit.com

Website of internationally acclaimed bullying prevention author, Barbara Coloroso.

www.rootsofempathy.org/Home.html

Roots of Empathy is an evidence-based classroom program that has shown dramatic effect in reducing levels of aggression and violence among school children while raising social/emotional competence and increasing empathy. Roots of Empathy has been identified as an anti-bullying program. Because children are taught to understand how others feel and are encouraged to take responsibility for their actions and inactions, pro-social behaviors rise and incidents of bullying and aggression fall.

www.nmmlp.org

The New Mexico Media Literacy Project, one of the oldest and most successful media literacy organizations in the United States, empowers children, youth, and adults to become more critical consumers of media messages.

www.thegraycenter.org

The Gray Center for Social Learning and Understanding is a non-profit, 501(c)(3) organization dedicated to individuals with autism spectrum disorders (ASD) and those who work alongside them to improve mutual understanding. It was founded by the well known creator of Social Stories, Carol Gray, who is also author of *Gray's Guide to Bullying*. The Gray Center approaches the social impairrment in ASD as a shared impairment. They work to improve social understanding on both sides of the social equation, helping individuals with ASD to communicate and interact more successfully with the people with whom they live and work. This website provides a wealth of information on ASDs.

References

Adolphs, R., Damasio, A.R., Damasio, H., and Tranel, D. (1995) "Fear and the human amygdala." *Journal of Neuroscience 15*, 5879–5891.

American Bar Association (2006) *Model Rules of Professional Conduct.* Rule 8.3. Chicago, IL: ABA.

American Psychiatric Association (2000) *Diagnostic and Statistical Manual of Mental Disorders IV-TR.* (Fourth Edition, Text Revision.) Washington, DC: American Psychiatric Association.

Arora, T. (1991) "The Use of Victim Support Groups." In P.K. Smith and D. Thompson (eds) *Practical Approaches to Bullying.* London: David Fulton.

Asperger, H. (1991) "Autistic Psychopathy in Childhood." (U. Frith, trans., annot.). In U. Frith (ed.) *Autism and Asperger Syndrome.* New York, NY: Cambridge University Press. (Original work published in 1944.)

Aston, M. (2003) *Aspergers in Love: Couple Relationships and Family Affairs.* London: Jessica Kingsley Publishers.

Attwood, T. (1998) *Asperger Syndrome: A Guide for Parents and Professionals.* London: Jessica Kingsley Publishers.

Attwood, T. and Gray, C. (1999) "The Discovery of 'Aspie' Criteria." *The Morning News 11*, 3. Retrieved from www.thegraycenter.org/sectionsdetails.cfm?id=38. Also available at www.tonyattwood.com.au

Baron-Cohen, S. and Craig, J. (1999) "Creativity and imagination in autism and Asperger Syndrome." *Journal of Autism and Developmental Disorders 29*, 4, 319–326.

Beane, A. (1999) *A Bully Free Classroom: Over 100 Tips and Strategies for Teachers K-8.* Minneapolis, MN: Free Spirit Publishing, Inc.

Besag, V.E. (1989) *Bullies and Victims in School.* Milton Keynes: Open University Press.

Bogdashina, O. (2005) *Communication Issues in Autism and Asperger Syndrome.* London: Jessica Kingsley Publishers.

Boulton, M.J. and Smith, P.K. (1994) "Bully/victim problems in middle-school children; stability, self-perceived competence, peer perceptions and peer acceptance." *British Journal of Developmental Psychology 12*, 315–329.

Brooks, F., Bartini, M., and Pellegrini, A.D. (1999) "School bullies, victims and aggressive victims: factors relating to group affiliation and victimization in early adolescence." *Journal of Education Psychology 91*, 216–224.

Brown, J.M., O'Keefe, J., Sanders, S.H., and Baker, B. (1986) "Developmental changes in children's cognition to stressful and painful situations." *Journal of Pediatric Psychology 11*, 343–357.

Center for Disease Control and Prevention (2007) *Autism Spectrum Disorders Overview.* Atlanta, GA: Center for Disease Control and Prevention. Retrieved from www.cdc.gov/ncbddd/autism/overview.htm

Cohen, D.J., Klin, A., and Schultz, R.T. (1999) "The Need for a Theory of Theory of Mind in Action: Developmental and Neurofunctional Perspectives in Social Cognition." In S. Baron-Cohen, D. Cohen, and H. Tager-Flusberg (eds) *Understanding Other Minds* (second edition). Oxford: Oxford University Press.

Coloroso, B. (2003) *The Bully, the Bullied and the Bystander: From Preschool to High School—How Parents and Teachers Can Help Break the Cycle of Violence.* New York, NY: HarperResource (An Imprint of HarperCollins Publishers).

Craig, W.M. and Pepler, D.J. (1995) "Peer Processes in Bullying and Vicitimzation: An Observational Study." *Exceptionality Education Canada, 5,* 81–95.

Dauber, H. and Fox, J. (1999) *Gathering Voices: Essays on Playback Theatre.* New Paltz, NY: Tusitala Publishing.

Davies, A. (2004) *Teaching Asperger Students Social Skills Through Acting: All Their World's a Stage!* Arlington, TX: Future Horizons.

Davis, S. (2005) *Schools Where Everyone Belongs: Practical Strategies for Reducing Bullying.* Champaign, IL: Research Press.

Delfos, M. (2005) *A Strange World—Autism, Asperger Syndrome and PDD-NOS: A Guide for Parents, Partners, Professional Carers and People with ASDs.* London: Jessica Kingsley Publishers.

Dubin, N. (2004) *Diagnosis Asperger: Nick Dubin's Journey of Self-Discovery.* Kentwood, MI: Gray Center Publications.

Dyer, W. (2004) *The Power of Intention: Learning to Co-create Your World Your Way.* Carlsbad, CA: Hay House Inc.

Dziuba-Leatherman, J. and Finkelhor, D. (1994) "The victimization of children: a development perspective." *American Psychologist 49,* 173–183.

Eron, L.D. (1986) "Interventions to mitigate the psychological effects of media violence on aggressive behavior." *Journal of Social Issues 42,* 155–169.

Evans, R., Ewbank, R., Fonagy, P., Giels, M.L, Sacco, P., and Twemlow, S. (2001) "Creating a peaceful school learning environment: a controlled study of an elementary school intervention to reduce violence." *American Journal of Psychiatry 158,* 808–810.

Fay, J. and Funk, D. (1995) *Teaching with Love and Logic: Taking Control of the Classroom.* Golden, CO: The Love and Logic Press, Inc.

Fennell, T. (1993) "Fear in the hallways." *Maclean's 106,* 19.

Fried, S. and Fried, P. (1996) *Bullies and Victims.* New York: M. Evans and Company, Inc.

Furniss, C. (2000) "Bullying in schools: It's not a crime—is it?" *Education and the Law 12,* 10–29.

Garry, E. and Grossman, J. (1997) *Mentoring—A Proven Delinquency Prevention Strategy.* Washington DC: U.S Department of Justice, Office of Juvenile Justice and Delinquency Prevention.

Gillberg, C. (2002) *A Guide to Asperger Syndrome.* Cambridge: Cambridge University Press.

Gilmartin, B.G. (1987) "Peer group antecedents of severe love-shyness in males." *Journal of Personality 55,* 467–489.

Glynn, T. and Wheldall, K. (1989) *Effective Classroom Learning.* Oxford: Blackwell.

Goldbloom, R. (2001) "Parents' primer on school bullying." *Reader's Digest Canada,* October, 6.

Gordon, M. (2005) *Roots of Empathy: Changing the World Child by Child.* Markham, Ontario: Thomas Allen and Son Limited.

Gray, C. (2003) "Gray's guide to bullying." *Jenison Autism Journal 16,* 1, 1–60.

Gray, J. and Sime, N. (1989) "Findings from the National Survey of Teachers in England and Wales." In Department of Education and Science, *Discipline in Schools: Report of the Committee of Inquiry Chaired by Lord Elton.* London: HMSO.

Hamer, D. (1994) *The Science of Desire: The Search for the Gay Gene and the Biology of Behavior.* New York, NY: Simon and Schuster.

Hartup, W.W. (1996) "The company they keep: friendships and their developmental significance." *Child Development 67,* 1–13.

Hawkins, G. (2004) *How to Find Work That Works for People with Asperger Syndrome: The Ultimate Guide for Getting People with Asperger Syndrome into the Workplace (and Keeping Them There).* London: Jessica Kingsley Publishers.

Hazler, R.J., Hoover, J.H., and Oliver, R. (1993a) "What do kids say about bullying?" *Education Digest 58,* 16–20.

Hazler, R.J., Hoover, J.H., Oliver, R.J., and Thompson, K.A. (1993b) "Perceived victimization by school bullies: New research and future direction." *Journal of Humanistic Education and Development 32,* 76–86.

Heinrichs, R. (2003) *Perfect Targets: Asperger Syndrome and Bullying—Practical Solutions for Surviving the Social World.* Shawnee Mission, KS: Autism Asperger Publishing Company.

Henault, I. (2005) *Asperger Syndrome and Sexuality: From Adolescence through Adulthood.* London: Jessica Kingsley Publishers.

Hoover, J.H. and Oliver, R.J. (1996) *The Bullying Prevention Handbook: A Guide for Principals, Teachers and Counselors.* Bloomington, IN: National Educational Service.

Jackson, L. (2002) *Freaks, Geeks and Asperger Syndrome: A User Guide to Adolescence.* London: Jessica Kingsley Publishers.

Katz, A.H. (1993) *Self Help in America: A Social Movement Perspective.* New York: Twayne.

Kirby, D. (2001) "What makes a bully?" *The Advocate,* July, 31–34.

Klin, A., Sparrow, S., and Volkmar, F. (2000) *Asperger Syndrome.* New York: The Guilford Press.

Kochenderfer, B.J. and Ladd, G.W. (1996) "Peer victimization: cause or consequence of school maladjustment?" *Child Development 67,* 1305–1317.

Konstantareas, M. (2005) "Anxiety and Depression in Children and Adolescents with Asperger Syndrome." In K. Stoddart (ed.) *Children, Youth and Adults with Asperger Syndrome.* London: Jessica Kingsley Publishers.

Lawson, W. (2005) *Sex, Sexuality and the Autism Spectrum.* London: Jessica Kingsley Publishers.

Lazarus, A.A. and Wolpe, J. (1966) *Behavior Therapy Techniques.* Oxford: Pergamon Press.

Ledgin, N. (2002) *Asperger's and Self-Esteem: Insight and Hope through Famous Role Models.* Arlington, TX: Future Horizons.

LeDoux, J. (1996) *The Emotional Brain: The Mysterious Underpinnings of Emotional Life.* New York, NY: Simon and Schuster.

Little, L. (2002) "Middle-class mothers' perceptions of peer and sibling victimization among children with Asperger Syndrome and nonverbal learning disorders." *Issues Comprehensive Pediatric Nursing 25*, 43–47.

Mahdavi, J. and Smith, P.K. (2002) "The operation of a bully court and perception of its success." *School Psychology International 23*, 327–341.

Maines, B. and Robinson, G. (1992) *Stamp out Bullying: Never Mind the Awareness, What Can We Do?* Portishead: Lame Duck Publishing.

Marr, N. and Field, T. (2001) *Bullycide: Death at Playtime.* Oxford: Success Unlimited.

McTaggart, L. (2003) *The Field: The Quest for the Secret Force of the Universe.* New York: Harper Paperbacks.

Menesini, E. and Modiano, R. (2002) "A Multi-faceted Reality: A Report from Italy." In. P.K. Smith (ed.) *Violence in Schools: The Response in Europe.* London: Routledge.

Moneymaker, J. (1991) "Animals and inmates: a sharing companionship behind bars." *Journal of Offender Rehabilitation 16*, 133–153.

Olweus, D. (1991) "Bully/victim problems among school children: basic facts and effects of a school-based intervention program." In D. Pepler and K. Rubin (eds) *The Development and Treatment of Childhood Aggression.* Hillsdale, NJ: Erlbaum.

Olweus, D. (1993) *Bullying at School: What We Know and What We Can Do.* Oxford: Blackwell Publishers.

O'Malley, B. (1993) "Screening out the bullies." *Times Educational Supplement Resources,* June, 15.

Ozonoff, S. and Griffith, E.M. (2000) "Neuropsychological function and the External Validity of Asperger Syndrome." In A. Klin, F.R. Volkmar and S.S. Sparrow (eds) *Asperger Syndrome.* New York, NY: Guilford Press.

Palmer, A. (2006) *Realizing the College Dream with Autism or Asperger Syndrome: A Parent's Guide to Success.* London: Jessica Kingsley Publishers.

Pearsall, P. (1999) *The Heart's Code: Tapping the Wisdom and Power of Heart Energy.* New York, NY: Broadway Books.

Perry, D.G., Perry, L.C., and Kusel, S.J. (1988) "Victims of peer aggression." *Developmental Psychology 24*, 807–814.

Pert, C. (1997) *Molecules of Emotion: Why You Feel the Way You Do.* New York, NY: Scribner (A division of Simon and Schuster).

Peterson, L. and Rigby, K. (1999) "Countering bullying at an Australian secondary school." *Journal of Adolescence 22*, 481–492.

Pikas, A. (1989) "The Common Concern Method for the Treatment of Mobbing." In E. Munthe and E. Roland (eds) *Bullying: An International Perspective.* London: Fulton.

Prothrow-Stith, D. (1991) *Deadly Consequences.* New York, NY: HarperCollins.

Ritchey, K. (2006) "Orton-Gillingham and Orton-Gillingham based reading instruction: A review of the literature." *The Journal of Special Education 40*, 171–183.

Ross, D.M. (1984) "Thought-stopping: a coping strategy for impending feared events." *Issues in Comprehensive Pediatric Nursing 7*, 83–89.

Ross, D.M. (2003) *Childhood Bullying, Teasing and Violence: What School Personnel, Other Professionals and Parents Can Do* (second edition). Alexandria, VA: American Counseling Association.

Ross, D.M. and Ross, S.A. (1988) *Childhood Pain: Current Issues, Research and Management.* Baltimore, MD: Urban and Schwarzenburg.

Seligman, M.E.P. (1975) *Helplessness: On Depression, Development and Death.* San Francisco, CA: Freeman.

Smith, P.K., Sutton, J., and Swettenham, J. (1999) "Social cognition and bullying: social inadequacy or skilled manipulation?" *British Journal of Developmental Psychology 17,* 435–450.

Smith, P.K. and Whitney, I. (1993) "A survey of the nature and extent of bullying in junior/middle and secondary school." *Educational Research 35,* 1, 3–25.

Stillman, W. (2006) *Autism and the God Connection: Redefining the Autistic Experience Through Extraordinary Accounts of Spiritual Giftedness.* Naperville, IL: Sourcebooks Inc.

Sylvia, C. (1997) *A Change of Heart.* New York, NY: Warner Books.

Tantam, D. (1991) "Asperger Syndrome in Adulthood." In U. Frith (ed.) *Autism and Asperger Syndrome.* Cambridge: Cambridge University Press.

Williams, D. (2003) *Exposure Anxiety—The Invisible Cage: An Exploration of Self-Protection Responses in the Autism Spectrum and Beyond.* London: Jessica Kingsley Publishers.

Wing, L. (2001) *The Autistic Spectrum: A Parents' Guide to Understanding and Helping Your Child.* Berkeley, CA: Ulysses Press.

Wolff, S. (1995) *Loners: The Unusual Life Path of Unusual Children.* London and New York: Routledge.

Young, M. (1998) *Learning the Art of Helping.* Upper Saddle Rv, NJ: Prentice Hall Inc.

Index

The following DVD by Nick Dubin is available from Jessica Kingsley Publishers:

Being Bullied
Strategies and Solutions for People with
Asperger's Syndrome
ISBN 978 1 84310 843 6

Bullying is a serious problem in schools and children on the autism spectrum are particularly at risk of being victimized if they display "different" behavior, such as not understanding rules, having bad handwriting or flapping their hands.

Being Bullied describes the various types of peer abuse —taunting, nicknames, damaging property, stealing, and cyber bullying—and the devastating consequences, such as poor self-esteem, low academic achievement, depression, or even suicide.

Narrated by Nick Dubin and featuring footage of his own childhood that illustrates behaviors that made him an easy target for bullies, the film also includes the stories of three individuals with Asperger's Syndrome who talk about their experiences of being bullied.

The DVD outlines practical strategies for parents, professionals, schools, and individuals being bullied on how to prevent bullying. It stresses the importance of peer intervention, empathetic teachers, and verbal self-defense and shows how lack of teacher support, condemning of "tale telling," or even blaming the victim reinforces bullying.

This DVD offers children and young people who are being bullied a chance to see that they are not alone, and will be a valued source of advice for parents and professionals.

Order this DVD online via our website: www.jkp.com